A Very Special Place

BY THE SAME AUTHOR

The Authorized Version: The Biography of Ronnie Wallace
Flings Over Fences: The Ups and Downs of Guy Kindersley

AS CO-AUTHOR

Irish Hussar: A History of the Queen's Royal Irish Hussars
(with Tim Pierson and John Strawson)
Loopy: The Autobiography of Sir George Kennard
(with Sir George Kennard)

A VERY SPECIAL PLACE

Tales from the Goring Hotel

Robin Rhoderick-Jones

Illustrated by

Tim Jaques

THE GORING HOTEL
London

First published in 1997 by
The Goring Hotel
Beeston Place
Grosvenor Gardens
London SW1W OJW

Edited, designed and produced for
The Goring Hotel by
Gun Room Publishing
10 Chamberlain Street
Regent's Park Road
London NW1 8XB

ISBN 0 9529599 0 9

A CIP record for this book is available from the British Library

Typeset by Mel-Art Graphics
Printed by Midas Printing Limited
Colour origination by Wace Publication Imaging, London

Contents

ACKNOWLEDGEMENTS

Writing this book has been a particular pleasure, and the word 'acknowledgements' is wholly inadequate to describe the debt I owe to those who have made my task such fun.

First among them are George and Penny Goring, whose idea it was. Their enthusiasm, generosity and consideration to me mirrored in full measure the way in which George runs his hotel – smoothly, without fuss, efficiently but never officiously and, above all, with the needs of the Goring's patrons always the first priority. Thanks to George's organizational skills, I was able to interview dozens of his staff, both past and present, gathered at my convenience during the many days I spent doing research, and all without any apparent interruption in the hotel's real work. To those staff, far too many to list individually, I offer my thanks for their time, their company and their incredible memories.

My thanks too, to Edna, Mrs OG Goring, who, for over sixty years as daughter-in-law, wife and mother has been such a rock-like support to the three members of her family who have, as it were, had their names above the door. I am very grateful to her for the historical perspectives she supplied and the patience with which she answered my doubtless impertinent questions.

Our advertisements in national newspapers in this country and the United States, inviting reminiscences from guests of the Goring, produced an avalanche of responses, all of which have been acknowledged individually. It has not been possible to include even extracts from more than a fraction of them, but I am grateful none the less to all those who wrote, and have protected the anonymity of those who requested it.

I offer particular thanks to Toby Buchan, my editor, for his patient work and always helpful suggestions, and finally to Tim Jaques, who has adorned these pages with the brilliant illustrations that have brought my text and its characters to life in a way that words could never achieve. I thank Tim, too, for designing the layout and arranging the publication. I am lucky indeed to have had him on board.

ROBIN RHODERICK-JONES
Middle St Andrew's Wood, 1997

In the Beginning . . .

As rich as Croesus . . . This last native-born king of Lydia ruled his country, in what is now Turkey, for fourteen years until, in 546 BC, he was overthrown by the Persian, Cyrus the Great. Croesus was rich because he had gold. Gold in such quantities that his mines yielded up practically all that was then known within the ancient civilizations of Asia Minor. The Lydians put their rare and precious metal to good use, fashioning decorative artefacts and, more importantly – when they came to understand that their bountiful gods had provided them with a treasure much sought after by all who had seen (or even merely heard) of it – turning quantities of the stuff into small flat discs decorated with the heads of their kings. In short the Lydians invented money.

The idea caught on. Soon every nation state with any pretensions to power and riches was producing coins from whatever intrinsically valuable metal was available, and this revolutionary method of wealth exchange remained unaltered for hundreds of years, facilitating trade and robbery in equal measure, and giving rise to a whole new criminal fraternity as enterprising forgers realized that anyone with a modicum of talent as a metal-worker, and a modest source of the appropriate raw material, could turn himself into a bank. It was the Chinese who eventually produced paper money as a practical alternative, an innovation which quickly developed into the modern system of national currencies – a system which was, however, still entirely underpinned by gold in financially important countries until the gold standard was finally abandoned in 1931.

As money became generally acceptable as a means of paying for goods and rewarding service, the urge to travel in order to trade gathered momentum, and with it came the need of travellers for lodging. In those early days an inn was little more than a portion of a private dwelling: largely self-service, rarely clean, and usually run by a disreputable landlord. In England, it was not until the Industrial Revolution of the late eighteenth century onwards that there began to be welcome signs of progress. In response to demand, innkeepers added to the services available, made an effort to maintain some sort of standard of cleanliness, and even began to cater to the particular needs of their guests. For over a century from around 1750, English inns gained the reputation of being the finest in the world, as roads were improved and the new ideas spread to the provinces. But, with few exceptions, the hostelries still remained small and generally ill-favoured until, in 1865 the Langham Hotel was built in Portland Place – the first of the capital's grand establishments. Opened with appropriate pomp and circumstance by the Prince of Wales (later King Edward VII), it was the largest building in the capital. Despite the Langham's opulence, however, England could not compete with similar developments across the Atlantic Ocean.

Beginning with the Tremont House in Boston (which predated the Langham by over thirty years and enabled the latter to copy its innovations) the architect Isaiah Rogers did away with the inn-like policy of providing large sleeping rooms having anything from two to ten beds, designing his hotels to incorporate only single and double bedrooms. Rogers's design caught the American public's imagination and for fifty years he traded successfully on the desire of each big city across the newly united country to outdo its neighbours in the grandeur and lavishness of its hotels. The demand in America appeared almost insatiable and the industry grew far more quickly there than in Europe, the essential difference being that European hotels in the nineteenth century operated on the premise that they existed solely for the comfort and wellbeing of the travelling aristocracy, whereas in the more egalitarian climate of the United States the demand was widely spread. Quite simply, the average American got about more, so much so that by 1900 the luxury market had been superseded by a clamorous demand for cheaper and more functional – so-called 'commercial' – hotels to cater for the less affluent.

In England, change came at a pace considerably more sedate. The rise of a moneyed upper-middle-class anxious to assume the trappings of aristocracy opened the eyes of hoteliers to the possibility of providing, in the cities, an environment which would reproduce the atmosphere of an English country house. But British businessmen – focused almost entirely on making money by manufacturing goods for the rest of the world – were slow to grasp the opportunity. It was left to the Continentals to seize the initiative, so that even those few British-owned grand hotels among the many which began to spring up in London were largely staffed and managed by German, French and Italian entrepreneurs expert in providing an excellence to which the English found it difficult to aspire. The greatest hotels in London established their enviable worldwide reputations for providing British standards of service almost solely under the guidance of foreigners.

For the first fifty years of the twentieth century, London's grandest and most exclusive hotels maintained their independence. But, as the world emerged from the economic shadows of the Second World War and its austere aftermath, one by one they began to fall prey to national and international conglomerates, some of which had little or no previous experience of the industry. Soon most of these hotels became a sort of standard product, indistinguishable from those establishments which joined their ranks in the misjudged explosion of luxury accommodation in the capital during the tourist boom of the 1980s. A few, a very few, clung tenaciously to the qualities which had made them special: their size, their tradition of service in the manner of that found in the great private houses of England, and their insistence on treating every guest as a cherished individual to be cared for as a member of a well-respected family. Among them, and perhaps the most English of all, is one of which it may be said, as did *The Times* of 30 May 1990: 'The Goring is the most distinguished London hotel still in private ownership.'

This is its story.

1 *The Founder's Tale*

The Kaiser was miffed. Stiff-necked and scowling, he marched slowly out of Westminster Hall at the shoulder of his cousin, King George V. Following them as they set off on the long journey to Paddington station trailed a phalanx of the crowned heads of Europe: the Kings of Belgium, Bulgaria, Denmark, Greece, Norway, Portugal and Spain, and, somewhere down among the lesser but still royal mortals, the Archduke Franz Ferdinand of Austria-Hungary, whose fatal encounter with a Serbian bullet on the streets of Sarajevo four years later was to ignite the world in war.

Wilhelm II was satisfied enough with his place at the head of this blue-blooded procession. His ill temper stemmed solely from the irksome fact that in front – between him and the gun-carriage bearing the body of his uncle, the late Edward VII, King of England – trotted a small dog. The Kaiser was not fond of dogs, and this one in particular had done nothing to endear himself to the German emperor. Indeed, he had constantly irritated Wilhelm in the past, when Emperor and

King-Emperor had met, by attempting to bite him on sight – incidents which had never failed to afford the now departed King Edward much ill-concealed amusement. Caesar the fox terrier, oblivious of the resentment aimed at his erect tail but still wondering, after two months, why his master no longer fed him, gazed disconsolately at the crowds as he allowed the kilted Highlander at his side to set the stately pace.

Standing among the half-million mourning subjects lining the streets, Otto Richard Goring smiled to himself. He had

much to smile about. A few weeks earlier he had realized his lifelong dream by opening in London the first hotel in the world to provide its guests with a private bath with every bedroom, while at the same time keeping them warm by means of radiators fuelled by a magnificent new-fangled boiler in the basement. The Ritz, Claridge's, Brown's, White's and now the Goring – Otto Richard had joined the distinguished and eponymous ranks of London's great hotel owners.

He had not been born an Englishman, although his and other families bearing the name had been in the service of the kings of England some five hundred years earlier. In the fourteenth century Edward III had employed an elite corps of mercenary pike-bearers whom he called the Goeringers after the area of the small German state from which they were recruited. Since that time Goerings (or Görings), Gorings and Geerings had settled in the south-east of England, assuming an Englishness which had led their descendant Lord George Goring, Earl of Norwich and favourite of King James I, to build Goring House on the site of the present Buckingham Palace. Some of the families had continued to spawn soldiers of fortune, among them a distinguished officer in Wellington's army who had chased Napoleon all the way to Moscow in 1812 before losing a leg and eventually settling in Saxony.

It was there that Otto Richard was born in 1869 and was soon to acquire an early ambition to make his way in the hotel industry which then – in Europe at least – catered almost exclusively for the aristocracy. In 1899, while working at the smartest hotel in the Grand Duchy of Saxe-Weimar-Eisenach, he had first made the acquaintance of the then Crown Prince of Germany – the very same man whose upstaged discomfort he was now witnessing. Goring had been a waiter at the time, and engaged in serving Wilhelm and a noisy party of friends with lavish quantities of the champagne strawberry cup of which they were so demonstrably fond. He and his fellow servants, making the most of a rare opportunity, were able to spirit away more than the usual number of half-empty bottles, refreshing themselves so liberally that when he at last went up to bed at the very top of the hotel he was sick out of his window. Up early the next morning and still feeling far from well, Otto was slowly laying the Crown Prince's breakfast on the royal balcony three floors below when he was horrified to discover that the boxes of geraniums which lined the balustrade seemed to have sprouted strawberries. Wilhelm emerged from his suite and watched the young man's painstaking efforts to remove the half digested fruit. 'Ah, yes', he said. 'I, too, have observed that these flowers seem to have grown many berries during the night.'

A year later, in 1890, Otto Goring, in determined pursuit of further top-class experience, was at the famous old

Frankfurterhof, a favourite resting-place of the Prince of Wales during his frequent European tours, and had been placed in charge of that distinguished guest's breakfast table. Shortly after Edward had begun to tuck into dishes piled high with cold venison, eggs and cheeses which in those days gave the term 'Continental breakfast' an entirely more agreeable meaning than its modern derivative, the head waiter was aghast to see that his protégé was engaged in ushering a second visitor to the royal table. He remained frozen in anguish until this apparently monumental *faux pas* had run its course, and then took the young Otto aside. 'What,' he hissed, 'do you think you are doing, you idiot? That is the future King of England. How can you allow some lesser person to join him?' Otto was unmoved; his work in Weimar had given him a useful knowledge of the intricacies of blue-blooded genealogies. 'I have done nothing,' he replied, 'except to show the King of Bulgaria to his cousin's table.'

By 1893 Goring was in London, at that time the mecca of aspiring hoteliers, and employed as a banqueting waiter at the Hotel Metropole. This was a period characterized by gargantuan dinners, whose nine courses would be interspersed with lengthy and often saucy entertainments designed to allow the fashionable diners a welcome digestive break and give the chefs time to finish off their complicated dishes. The working nights were long and OR (he preferred to be known by his initials, perhaps to disguise a little his German origins at a time when relations between that country and Britain were becoming somewhat strained) was impatient to move up the professional ladder. By the end of the century he was managing a hotel near Southend and had married the slight, precise and well-bred Alice Tracy who was to tutor him through the otherwise inexplicable social pitfalls which awaited foreigners and who, even more importantly, was soon to bear him a son. Three years later he became a naturalized British subject, thereby giving practical expression to what was already an uncritical love for his adopted country and a deep-seated respect for the habits of its county gentry.

Bored with the east coast, he moved back to London and bought the old premises of the Naval and Military Club in South Kensington. Having redecorated the shabby rooms, he opened it as the Harrington Hotel, aiming at the genteel clientele made up of the many retired military and diplomatic families living on small pensions. OR was now the proprietor of his own establishment, but was still far from satisfying his ambitions. Within two years he had acquired the Cromwell Hotel, not far away in Thurloe Place, and placed it under management.

In both these enterprises his fertile and far-reaching plans to become a leading hotelier were frustrated by the limitations of the old-fashioned buildings he occupied. He was also rapidly becoming disenchanted with the constant haggling over prices to which his impoverished residents subjected him. Over the next few years, therefore, he looked around, coming eventually to the conclusion that he was too far away from the real scene of fashionable action. His researches persuaded him that the area of Westminster around Grosvenor Gardens offered a golden opportunity to start afresh. Whether by luck or prescient sound judgement – probably a combination of both – OR had, as it turned out, backed a winner. Victoria was ripe for development: the partially completed railway station was destined to become the major terminus for Continental traffic and, just as crucially, leading companies were looking for head offices away from the already overcrowded City.

Fronting Ebury Street, between the discreet middle-class Victoria Square and the narrow little Eaton Lane, were sixty slum properties whose leases had fallen in. A recession made the speculative acquisition of such a site an attractive proposition, and OR negotiated a new let from the Duke of Westminster's Grosvenor Estates, which owned the property. On it he built his hotel – some fifty bedrooms on four floors, each with its own bathroom, each centrally heated, while on every level were set copper piping outlets into which the maids could plug in hoses with hydraulically operated vacuum attachments that sucked up dust and small debris, delivering these unwanted items not, as might be expected, to some vast Hoover bag in the basement, but straight into London's main sewers. Nor were these alone among the innovations which were to secure for the Goring its ranking as the best-equipped hotel in London. In the front hall stood a telephone exchange connected by house lines to each room, so that guests could communicate directly with the management and be summoned to external phones, one on each floor, to take outside calls. The public rooms, opening off this hall and set over the kitchens, overlooked the raised and enclosed garden which had been created from the rubble of slum clearance – a further attraction which set the Goring apart from its less well-endowed competitors.

Not all ran smoothly, however. In this otherwise perfect embodiment of its owner's dreams, there was one feature which gave rise to more than the occasional twitch of unease: the lift had a mind of its own. Worked by hauling on a rope, it was enthusiastically embraced by the guests until they discovered how difficult it was to bring the thing to a halt at

the desired point of disembarkation. Frequently it overshot; just as often it stopped stubbornly short, obliging its passengers to negotiate a yawning gap. Worse, when it felt particularly playful it would take off without awaiting instructions and, exercising an independence not envisaged by its vexed owner, would suddenly stop between floors, resisting all attempts at retrieval until the manufacturers were called. Like any other unsuitable member of OR's team, it was soon to be replaced.

Close to Buckingham Palace and the American and Spanish Embassies in Grosvenor Gardens, the Goring Hotel was well situated to beguile comfort-seeking visitors from both home and abroad. On 1 March 1910 it welcomed its first guests as Colonel and Mrs Moore, up from Devon for a week, were delivered by growler from Paddington Station. They had come to a London which still largely depended on horses for both public and private transport. Growlers (enclosed cabs with room for four), hansoms (only two passengers, but speedier), and open-topped omnibuses patrolled the streets, the latter requiring a second horse to be added before negotiating the gradients from Victoria up to Hyde Park Corner and the Ritz in Piccadilly. The first underground railway line had recently been opened, but the small engines belching black smoke and drawing small ten-seater carriages, so coated their passengers in soot that, at the very least, a change of shirt was required after every trip. No potential guest of the Goring – and certainly not its fastidious proprietor – would have deigned to use them.

The Moores were greeted by a beaming OR and conducted by him to their room. This in itself was perhaps not surprising, in view of the significance of the occasion, but it was the first sign of the of the extraordinary level of personal service which was to distinguish the Goring in the years to come. Portly, with a rosy complexion, receding hair, bristly ginger moustache and twinkling blue eyes, OR's aspect was one for which the cliché 'genial host' might have been invented. Even before the advent of the Goring he had gained wide respect among London's leading hoteliers. Gelardi of the Savoy, Branchini at Claridge's, Heim of the Piccadilly, and Judah, the almost legendary manager of the Café Royal, were his friends, and he had already become a prominent figure in

the Réunion des Gastronomes, an exclusive society formed in 1899 by those who had reached the heights of the profession. Membership of this club was by invitation and, at the annual dinner, a leading chef would be invited to create a dish and have it appraised by the assembled grandees. Those in the know were now keen to sample what Mr Goring and his prestigious new venture had to offer.

At 7s 6d (about 37 pence nowadays, though in practice a very great deal more) for a single room and 12s 6d a double, the Goring was sought after from the day of its inception. During the years running up to the First World War its clientele was drawn largely from the English 'County Set', whose values and way of life had so impressed OR from the day he arrived in his adopted country. Many of the guests stayed for weeks, usually to coincide with the London Season; some became long-term residents, effectively making the hotel their only home, while for others it served as a London residence from which they would commute regularly to their houses in the country.

The Goring, in common with all London's grand hotels, employed a high proportion of foreign staff, drawn to work in London by the capital's well-merited reputation as an essential cog in the machinery of a serious career. All this changed, however, when, on 6 August 1914 – two days after the outbreak of war – the hotel's entire complement of German and French employees marched arm in arm to Victoria Station, to begin a journey that was to end in the trenches of Flanders, and with them on opposing sides. As they marched they sang their national anthems, the French giving an enthusiastic rendering of 'Deutschland über Alles' while the Germans solemnly belted out the 'Marseillaise'. This scene of touching naïvety, born out of the truly international nature of the industry's brotherhood, marked the end – arguably for ever – of the hitherto untrammelled flow of staff from across the Channel.

The abrupt disappearance of most of his workforce was far from the only problem that the war posed for OR and the still fledgeling Goring. The daily supply of food and drink became increasingly difficult to maintain as horses disappeared from the streets when they, too, were requisitioned for active service, the buses being replaced in time by the motorized vehicles of the the London General Omnibus Company. More serious still was the almost overnight evaporation of familiar guests as the social whirl rapidly wound down. For the first time, far too many of the Goring's rooms became, and then remained, empty. In and around Whitehall, hotels were being taken over to house departments of the expanding War Office – a salvation which, for nearly three long years, was to be denied to the Goring. When, however, the Americans entered the war in 1917, the situation improved. The *London Evening News* reported the event:

> Yet another West End hotel has been commandeered – the Goring Hotel, Grosvenor Gardens, one of the most select places in London. This afternoon official intimation was received that the hotel would be taken over by the Headquarters Staff of the Commander of the American troops in England. Mr Bassanetti, the manager, told *The Evening News* that several American officers have been staying there lately and the hotel, being so convenient for Victoria Station, is largely patronized by British officers home on leave.
>
> The fact that every bedroom is fitted with a telephone and radiator while a bath-room is attached may have had something to do with the choice. It is also quite close to the American Embassy.

Every movable item of furniture and equipment, including the kitchen ranges, was painstakingly labelled by OR himself before being carted off to a storage warehouse on the outskirts of the city. The gutted kitchens became the United States Army's communications centre for Europe, and direct lines were installed to connect the American Commander-in-Chief, General Pershing with President Woodrow Wilson. The garden, fountain and pond, only lately completed but already proving a draw for the rare breeds of duck cherished by King George V over the Palace wall a little to the north, became a barrack square and now resounded to unfamiliar words of command. The ducks went home.

In two important aspects, the Goring fared better than

most hotels from its peremptory commandeering and occupation. Once the war had ended – in November 1918 – the Americans wasted no time in dismantling their command structure in London, and the hotel became the first in England to be released from requisition and given back into its former ownership. Just as fortunately, the generals, in their anxiety to return home as quickly as possible, were not disposed to engage in petty arguments about compensation. Instead, they made good what remarkably little damage there was, redecorated the rooms to OR's not undemanding specifications, paid their remaining bills, and were gone. Other London establishments, subjected to the vacillating parsimony and endless red tape of the British War Office, were not so lucky.

OR now turned his attention to restoring to the Goring the days of prosperity which had marked its first four years. The crucial first step was to persuade the Duke of Westminster to part with the freehold – the property having been originally acquired on a ninety-nine-year-lease. OR prepared the negotiating ground carefully, but at first the Duke and his agents were unreceptive. Eventually, in the face of an avalanche of letters, and by then having, no doubt, an understandable desire to rid its offices of the persistent presence of Mr Goring, the Estate capitulated and sold not only the hotel and garden but the remaining houses between the hotel and Victoria Square as well. The price was £19,000 all up, and OR perceived that he had made a useful deal. Immediately he began to lay plans for expansion.

Occupancy rates were slow to climb back to the previously high levels, however, and this together with the need to recover from the privations of the war, led to a considerable hike in the hotel's prices. Double rooms now stood at 45 shillings, while set luncheons and dinners cost 4s 6d and 7s 6d respectively*. Patterns, however, had changed little: the Goring still depended for the most part on its late-spring, summer and autumn trade. Few guests appeared in the winter, as those not engaged in country sports began once again to disappear to the South of France, where they would stay until the beginning of the Season. May, June and July were the peak periods, the Goring being particularly popular with those going to

*Nominally, these amounts would be £2.25, 22½p., and 37½p. today. In real terms, however, they equate, roughly, to £135, £13.50, and £22.50, respectively.

Buckingham Palace for levées, presentations, investitures and garden parties. The hotel began to gain a reputation as a convenient annexe to the Palace, and this perceived proximity to royalty began to attract increasing numbers of monied Americans.

OR's plans for development were given practical expression in two major phases. As a first step he added an additional (fifth) floor – a feat of engineering which in itself became something of an architectural talking point. The existing fourth-floor roof was adjudged to be not strong enough to bear the necessary weight, with the result that the extra level had to be 'hung' from steel stanchions erected at each corner; the additional rooms were thus, in effect, built from the ceiling down. Secondly, in 1925, the whole building was extended sideways to take in the area occupied by the houses between it and Victoria Square. These included the corner house owned by a Chinese family who had unwittingly helped the process along, having already burrowed deeply into the sandy foundations to create extensive (and entirely unauthorized) cellars. The discovery of the sandy subsoil explained why Ebury Street, unlike the rest of London, had always been relatively free of the industrial smog which regularly choked the capital in the winter months. Fog clings to clay but fights shy of sand, so that when even the nearby Belgrave Square suffered from a 'pea-souper' which reduced visibility to five yards, OR's guests enjoyed only the most minor of inconveniences. This happy circumstance also meant that the sandy soil from the excavations could be sold at a sharp and unexpected profit, a windfall much appreciated by the businesslike Mr Goring.

By July 1926, and fortuitously just ahead of the General Strike of 4-12 May, the Goring Hotel, now double its original size, was at last free of the major upheavals through which it had struggled for the previous four years. OR felt that the time had come when he might relax a little. He was nearly fifty-seven and his now pre-eminent place in the profession was calling increasingly on his time. As a leading luminary of the International Hotel Managers' Association, he was obliged to attend meetings all over the world. Travel in those days was gracious, but decidedly slow – no excursion to the United

States, for example, could be undertaken in less than a month – and, apart from these business trips, he and Alice enjoyed journeys abroad for their own sake, taking frequent cures in the major spas of Germany and delighting in the winter sunshine of the South of France. To the Continent the Gorings always travelled by car, invariably a comfortable, black limousine of a sober, understated appearance. Not for OR (although he could well afford it) the more obvious luxury of a Rolls-Royce. Such ostentation, he was convinced, would serve only to suggest to his guests that the Goring's rates were fixed at a level that owed more to providing for its owner than for its clientele. His personal appearance also reflected this conscious, if entirely genuine, desire to present a solid and worthy aspect to the world, the very antithesis of old-fashioned values: homburg hat, dark overcoat with astrakhan collar and silver-topped cane were the accoutrements with which he invariably faced the world, putting them aside to reveal a classically tailored dark suit as he moved chattily around his hotel, greeting his guests. By this time he had acquired, through his wife, Nevil House and its small estate near Tatsfield in Kent. This further evidence of his success in absorbing completely the kind of Englishness to which he had aspired since his arrival from Germany, pleased him mightily, and he fulfilled his squirearchical duties with a will.

Although he had always employed a manager, at the Goring, OR was very much a hands-on proprietor. Little escaped him in the way of how the hotel and its services were presented, although he found it irksome to deal with the more mundane aspects of administrative minutiae. Now that the expansion of the hotel, the increased trade, his frequent absences abroad and his fondness for Tatsfield were all competing for his attention, he felt that the time had come for his son to take a leading role and relieve him of some of the more disagreeable burdens. First as Manager in 1924, and then as Managing Director two years later, Otto Gustave Goring began to take up the reins.

2 *The Magician's Tale*

On 3 March 1995 the Goring Hotel celebrated its eighty-fifth birthday. Three hundred people attended – black tie, long dresses, jewellery out of the bank – a pleasingly classless kaleidoscope of regular customers, high-spending clients, retired senior staff, current employees, and those guests staying at the hotel that night who were not otherwise engaged. Lords of the land, captains of industry, receptionists, porters, head waiters and secretaries mingling together in friendly animation; deference where good manners, old habits and training required it, but never a sign of servility. Champagne, a magnificent buffet supper served by a full complement of chefs – happy for once to be part of the sparkling scene above stairs – a birthday cake foursquare on its silver plinth and, presiding over all, the family Goring at ease with themselves and with these, their friends.

Such a celebration is held every five years, and this was the fifth at which George Goring had been required to make a speech. Despite his gregarious nature, OR's grandson does not find public speaking easy. His delivery is becomingly hesitant and his manner, for one who has climbed to the topmost branches of more than a few daunting trees, a trifle awkward. His speech might easily have been the very personification of the 'Boring Goring'. That it was not was because of the patent sincerity and self-deprecating humour with which he paid tribute to his father and grandfather. His father, he related, was often asked the secret of the Goring's success and always claimed that the hotel was run by magic – and 'if I explained it all to you, it wouldn't be magic would it? . . .'

Otto Gustave Goring was born in 1901. An only child, he was sent to school at Dover College where he became an outstanding athlete and a notable rugby player. His sporting achievements, however, failed to shield him from the xenophobic bullying inflicted on those who bore German-sounding names at a time when even his position as First Sea Lord was not enough to save Prince Louis Battenberg from unwilling resignation. Battenberg eventually anglicized his surname (Mountbatten is a direct translation); Gustave, however, following the example of his father, attempted to hide behind his initials. Despite his boyhood misery – or perhaps because of it – he determined to become a master of his profession and, even more so than his father, to gain entry into the ranks of the English gentry. In short, he would show them.

In 1919 he went for a time to the École Hôtelière in Lausanne, acknowledged to be the world leader in the teaching of hotel management. For the following four years he worked his way round Europe, serving apprenticeships as waiter, chef and receptionist, his stopping-off points reading like a *Debrett* of the hotel world: the Villars Palace, the Hôtel du Palais in Biarritz, the Prince des Galles in Monte Carlo, the Plaza-Athénée and Palais d'Orsay in Paris, and Claridge's in London. He put these experiences to good use, developing, with his father's full encouragement, a wide understanding of the international scene. In 1923 he went with OR to New York for a jamboree the like of which had never before been seen. More than two thousand hotel men from Europe and America gathered in the Commodore for a meeting of the International Hotel Alliance hosted by John McEntee Bowman, President of the Bowman Group, a coast to coast chain of the biggest and the best establishments in the land. Mr Bowman lived up to his showman's reputation, providing in his ballroom an astonishing circus, complete with performing lions, camels and horses, a full size big-top (requiring some twenty-five tons of sawdust), high-wire acts and clowns as well as an eight-course dinner – the whole being described by the goggle-eyed managing director of the Willard Hotel in Washington, DC, as 'the gosh-durnedest thing I ever did see'. It was all a far cry from Ebury Street – not least because the only drink provided was a pink-coloured lemonade. Even Mr Bowman was unable to beat Prohibition.*

That evening heralded the beginning of a three-week tour

*Under the 16th Amendment to the Constitution, 1919, and the Volstead Prohibition Act, 1920, the sale or consumption of all alcohol was made illegal throughout the United States, a response to years of lobbying by religious, temperance and other pressure groups. Public opinion eventually forced the repeal of these laws in 1933, by which time corruption had become rife among public officials and organized crime had grown rich and powerful on the back of sales of illicit ('bootleg') liquor.

of the United States for the delegates from abroad, during which OG secured for himself an appointment as the European correspondent for the *National Hotel Review of America*, a magazine for which he wrote assiduously for several years, reporting on developments and personalities on the eastern side of the Atlantic. His journalism, and his father's pre-eminent position in the industry, assured him of an early entry into the most influential circles of his profession, and he came to be much in demand at conferences and other gatherings. He was soon publishing articles on such diverse, and occasionally arcane, subjects as 'Thoughts on Breakfast' (profitable if done well), 'The Country Hotel in Europe' (be prepared and keep smiling), 'The Dog as a Guest – an Extra Problem' (don't take them) and 'Pushing Variety – Greater Public Interest and Profit May be Sought with New Dishes' (which included the intelligence that Belgian chickens have smaller heads and so provide more meat to the pound). Under the headline 'Banqueting Practice Here and There', published in 1928, he describes for his American readership the eating habits of Europeans:

> The question of the consumption of foodstuffs is a national trait largely dictated by climate. The heaviest eaters are the Russians followed by the Dutch and Germans. A second category of moderately large eaters are the British, French, Belgians, Czechs and Hungarians. Smaller eaters are the Spanish, Italians, Portuguese, Greeks and Turks. It will be seen that this list goes from North to South and this rule applies throughout the world. I suspect that the Canadian eats more than the New Yorker while the smallest eaters in America live in the southern states.

It would be surprising if Texans were to subscribe to this theory, but OG's example of a banquet that the Goring might provide at a cost of a guinea (21 shillings) bears out his view of the British appetite of the day.

CAVIARE
OYSTERS
CONSOMMÉ DOUBLE MADRILENE
CRÈME D'HOMMARD
FILET DE SOLE WALESKA
POULARDE DE BRESSE À LA PETIT DUC
HARICOTS VERTS FRAIS DE JERSEY
POMMES DAUPHINES
COMMICE SUCHARD
PARAIR DE FRIANDISES

He is careful, however, to point out in the article that all wines and liqueurs are charged extra, and adds that this doubles the receipts taken from each table. Publicity such as this helped to enhance the Goring's growing international reputation as a centre of excellence.

If OR had put the stamp of gentility and personal service on his hotel, it was OG who gave the Goring its air of quiet efficiency. For above all he was an able administrator and, despite that oft-repeated claim in later years that matters worked by magic, it was his careful attention to the minutest detail that ensured that complaints were so rare that guests returned again and again. Physically he resembled his father, and he also shared with OR a taste for the high life, a keen appreciation of food and wine (especially wine), and a driving desire to be deeply involved with the profession. In many ways, though, father and son were very different. Where OR was gregarious, and even pushily conscious of his place in the world, loving nothing better than entertaining his guests in the manner of a country-house host, OG was painfully shy and modest to a degree. He hated the chatty perambulations around the dining room forced upon him by his father, and he never talked about his writing – even his children were to remain unaware of the immense respect in which the hotel world held him until they were well into their thirties.

Goring, *père* and *fils*, ran the hotel as a team during a period when the English upper classes were trying grimly to hang on to the lifestyle they had been privileged to enjoy before the Great War. It was, however, a losing, if prolonged, battle, and the hotel found itself adapting to inevitable changes.

As forecast by OR, Victoria now housed an increasingly commercial population, so that the proportion of residential and long-term guests dropped, being replaced by businessmen staying for a few days and producing a new and considerable demand for lunches as they entertained their clients both in the public and in the private dining rooms. There was also something of a tourist explosion, particularly from America and the Dominions, a cosmopolitan flavour mirrored at the Goring by the employment of staff from the Continent – French chefs and Italian, Spanish and Portuguese waiters, all now requiring tiresome work permits, but brought in to supplement those, at this time, relatively few English men and women who found hotel work congenial. The war had done more than just kill or maim millions – in Britain, it had destroyed for ever an entire social order, and left thousands with a determination never to serve their supposed superiors again.

There were also changes in the Goring family's personal circumstances when, in 1933, OG married Edna Bradbury, the only daughter of a Sheffield building magnate. As a girl, Edna had been sent to finishing school in Berlin, and her mother would see her off from and meet her again at the Goring, where OR and his wife took a personal interest in this neat, attractive, dark-haired and serious young woman, seeing her as an eminently suitable match for their hard-working son. The marriage, which was to last for over forty years, got off to a tragic start when, only hours after the ceremony, OG and Edna were involved in a car crash on the Great North Road in which a passenger in the other vehicle (which had burst a tyre and veered into the Gorings' path) was killed. The newlyweds spent their first night as a married couple in hospital in Grantham – which was not at all what OG had had in mind.

At first, the younger Gorings lived in a suite of rooms in the hotel, and Elizabeth, their eldest child, was born in Room 114. OG, not expecting the baby's arrival quite so imminently had gone to an official dinner, leaving instructions with the nurse that he would sleep in Room 104 and should be called if necessary. On his return he found that 104 had been let, and therefore found another room in which to sleep. The nurse, unaware of this change, trotted along at three in the morning

to break the good news, announcing from the door that a beautiful daughter had been born. The astonished Frenchman who tumbled out of bed to receive this unexpected revelation could hardly take it all in: 'C'est impossible; beaucoup trop vite!'

Now that his son was engaged in ensuring the Goring succession, OR set about acquiring the adjoining No. 2

Victoria Square for the young family – a rather protracted negotiation which involved the previous owner being allowed to occupy the house until her death (which, as it turned out, came two years later). But by 1938 they had moved in – just in time for their twin boys, George and Richard, to be born there. It was a joy tempered by sadness, however, for in that same year Alice Goring died. For some time she had been suffering from such chronic diabetes that one of her legs had been amputated in what proved to be an only partially successful attempt to prolong her life. She suffered both the pain and the indignity with cheerful fortitude, allowing neither to prevent her travelling with OR each February to spend a few weeks in Monte Carlo, and certainly not to interfere with their regular excursions to the United States.

By the time of his mother's death OG had run the Goring for ten years as its Managing Director – although he had never been entirely free of the feeling that his father watched over him with an eye that was as penetrating as ever. Despite the frequent travel and the flamboyant lifestyle, OR was a hard taskmaster who allowed his son little real latitude. A frequent bone of contention between them was the spending of money. Where OG was careful, sometimes to the point of parsimony, for example in redecorating the rooms, OR insisted that only the best would do, and that the catalogue of distinguished guests and society weddings to which the hotel played host was a vindication of his determination to maintain a certain style even during the years of recession. Indeed, at the Coronation of King George VI in May 1937, the Goring had become an annexe to Buckingham Palace, providing a temporary home for a range of royal and political heads of state to such an extent that a direct telephone line had been installed between the two establishments, and the road outside the hotel cleared by the police of all save those staying there. Among the guests was the Crown Prince of Norway, who appeared particularly pleased, confiding in OG that he much preferred to stay at the Goring: 'I never have a bathroom to myself in Buckingham Palace!'

Whatever his love of Europe, OG cannot have been blind to the increasingly threatening signs from Germany, nor especially surprised when, in September 1939, Britain and her allies declared war on the country of his father's birth. The first days of the Second World War found the younger Goring in an advanced state of preparation against the expected onslaught of German bombers – and determined never to give best to the air forces of the fat Reichsmarschall who bore his ancestral name. He and some of the staff had already taken Air-Raid Precaution (ARP) and First Aid courses – the lurid predictions of which scared them far more than any of the events that followed – and they set up a shelter in the basement furnished with the contents of the vacated fifth-floor bedrooms. Employees began to leave as they were called to the colours and guests had evaporated so quickly that on the day of the British ultimatum to Germany, there were only six paying customers.

Those guests were soon to experience at first hand the exigencies of London under bombardment when a basket of incendiary bombs landed on the roof. OG, keen to put his training into action, rushed to the scene to supervise the staff, who were enthusiastically engaged in levering the burning devices into the street below, using long-handled shovels. Noticing that one of the bombs appeared to be in such an advanced state of conflagration that it would be dangerous to move it, he smothered the thing with sand. With a last and satisfied look at a job well done, he and his men returned to their duties, enjoying to the full the notion that they had defeated the Luftwaffe's first (and, as it happened, last) direct assault on their beloved hotel. They were not to savour their triumph for long. Thwarted by the sand from burning itself out in the air, OG's bomb worked its way through the ashphalt covering of the roof and was now attacking the floor below. The firefighting team reassembled, filled the bath with water, connected their stirrup pumps, and finished the job.

For the first three years of the war OG watched in anguish as the Goring's financial reserves dwindled almost to nothing. It was not until 1942 that life began to return to something approaching normality, as servicemen of many and varied nationality began to fill the empty rooms. Firewatching duties continued, and there were several near misses as first Buckingham Palace was damaged, and then a bank in Grosvenor Gardens took direct hits, the blast rocking the hotel

and scattering thousands of five-pound notes into a burst water main. Not a few found their way into the kitchens to be dried out by the solicitous chefs.

OG's wartime activities were not, however, simply confined to running his hotel and firewatching from the roof. In 1941 the London County Council called on the hotel, café and restaurant owners of the capital to be prepared to feed the citizens in an emergency. OG was appointed to head the

Westminster operation and compiled detailed plans of not only the kitchens in his area but of the transport which could be requisitioned and pressed into service to distribute food. The kitchens – all of which had to be visited and carefully assessed – ranged from grand establishments at the Savoy, Dorchester and Grosvenor House Hotels, to pull-ups for cabmen, while the transport he earmarked included lorries, handcarts and even stretchers – the last thought to be the only practical method of carrying food across bomb craters. In detailed work of this nature, he excelled, his talent for administration and improvisation resulting in the preparation of a model contingency plan which provided for 350,000 meals twice a day, more than twice the number that could be provided in the rest of London and its suburbs put together.

Improvisation was very much in evidence at the Goring, too, as the garden was given over to growing tomatoes, while at his homes in the country, first at Nevil House (which he sold in 1944) and then at Court Lodge, Wrotham, Edna turned her lawns and flowerbeds into kitchen gardens, providing fresh vegetables for the hotel throughout both the war and, later, during the seemingly endless period of rationing and ration books that followed its end in 1945. She even turned her hand to canning, producing a thousand tins of apricots, plums and cherries a year from her own trees.

It was during this period of considerable stress that OG developed the diabetes and heart trouble which were to plague him for the rest of his life, and which forced Edna (against her inclination) to play a more prominent role in the running of the Goring until relieved – at least in part – by the return from the war of the excellent Norman Pennington, who had been engaged as General Manager shortly before the outbreak. The children, now at school, spent most of their time at Court Lodge, while OG and Edna occupied one of the three houses which had been acquired in Victoria Square, commuting to the country as opportunity – and petrol rationing – allowed. OR, too, had fallen ill, and had been taken to Wrotham to be cared for by a team of nurses. In 1948 the old man died. For the first time, his son found himself in sole, but even now not always indisputable, charge.

During the succeeding fourteen years the senior staff at the Goring slowly became aware that their working lives were in the hands of a triumvirate. At the apex of this small triangle stood OG – no longer, since his father's death, known to his employees as Mr Gustave. He was now, firmly, *the* Mr Goring. Self-effacing and reserved in manner, and with an unbending perception of everyone's proper station in life, he presented a cold exterior to those who worked for him. No one, not even Norman Pennington, dared to wish him 'good morning' until he had spoken first and he invariably addressed every member of staff – man and woman – by his or her surname. Other than the hotel industry, his absorbing passion was money and, in particular, its accumulation. He turned meanness into a minor art form and revelled in the reputation he knew he thereby enjoyed. 'I know you think I'm tight-fisted,' he would often say to his secretary, Edwina Davy. 'I don't think it – I know it, Mr Goring,' she would equally invariably reply, causing him to chuckle contentedly to himself. He spent hours each day poring over the *Financial Times* and telephoning the banks to check on the latest currency exchange rates, while his reluctance to spend what he considered to be outrageous sums in redecorating his hotel drove both his wife and his manager to adopt extremes of deviousness in their attempts to maintain standards. After months of argument, during which they had attempted to persuade OG that the ladies' lavatory needed

extensive refurbishment, he gave in and told them to get on with it: 'I never go down there, anyway'. Edna and Norman Pennington went to work with a will, ordering the plushest of materials and assigning the hotel's own painter and carpenter to the project as his first priority. One day, however, noticing that he hadn't seen the painter for a fortnight, OG made enquiries, to be told that the man was in the Ladies'. Venturing through the suspiciously new-looking door, he was appalled at the sight that presented itself: deep-pile carpets, curtains from Harrods, hand-made looking-glasses and gold taps were everywhere. This far from accorded with his own ideas of proper expenditure. Flying into a rage, he ordered the work to be undone: 'Take the carpet up; what's wrong with stone floors? – they're much easier to clean; whitewash the walls; send the curtains back'. Pennington reported this outburst to Edna, who characteristically countermanded her husband's instructions. The battle raged for days until – as he always did

when confronted by his implacable wife – OG gave way and the Goring acquired a ladies' lavatory to die for. But for a month the female guests had to make do with an upstairs bedroom.

It is perhaps surprising, given OG's autocratic ways, that his hotel worked so well and with such distinction. The key lay in the attitude of the staff – and particularly that of the more senior and longer-serving members. To a man and woman, they loved the Goring and its ethos of always putting the guests first. It was a notion imbued in them to such an extent that they, too, felt special in being a part of a team which prided itself on the very highest standards, taking such an interest in each customer that index cards were kept which detailed the background and personal foibles of individual guests. This attention to detail was not merely the result of edicts issued from above, however; the staff respected their Mr Goring and wanted his ways to work, admiring him for his professionalism, and appreciating his sincerity – for despite OG's distant demeanour and stiff formality, they knew where they stood with him and, more importantly, they also knew that a grievance would be considered with a scrupulous impartiality and an immediacy which was hard to come by in other establishments.

Like his father before him, OGs had wider hotel interests which tended to remove him more and more from the routine administration of the Goring. Shortly after the war he had resurrected, with Hugh Wontner of the Savoy, the International Hotel Association. He was also playing leading roles in a number of other bodies: the Hotel and Restaurants Association, the Hotel and Catering Institute and the Réunion des Gastronomes, as well as being a Freeman of the City of London and a Liveryman of the Worshipful Company of Clockmakers, the Worshipful Company of Distillers and the Worshipful Company of Bakers. Nor had his business acumen deserted him. In 1952 he bought the Coburg Hotel in Bayswater, which he turned into one of the first important company training and conference venues in London, before selling it six years later at an astonishing profit.

The other two corners of the ruling triangle were made up by Norman Pennington and Edna. The former effectively ran the Goring – although he was always careful to refer any major decision to the owner – while Edna, who had had some training in interior design, saw to the decoration and the furnishings, wringing the required funds out of her always reluctant husband. Edna was, however, far more than just an unpaid assistant. During OG's terms of office as President of this and Chairman of that, she was always at his side, encouraging him in his work and ensuring that his self-effacing nature was not imposed upon when it came to seats at the top table or precedence in the order in which speeches were made. She recognized her husband's worth to the international hotel industry, and was determined that his advice should be heard and his valuable experience not taken lightly. Above all, she watched over his health as his strength ebbed and flowed with advancing years. Of particular concern were the onset of diabetes and his increasing devotion to the bottle. For OG liked to drink. It was, of course, a hazard of his profession – his official duties often entailed attendance at a dozen or so functions a week – but his general physical state had left him ill-equipped to cope with such excesses. Edna, in a permanent state of loving anxiety, cared for him and saw to it that he received the very best of medical attention. In 1962 he was joined at the Goring by his son George, already carefully schooled in the business and enthusiastically ready to play his part. Father and son, despite the differences in management philosophies that were to become apparent, made a fine team as George came for the first time to recognize and appreciate with not a little wonder the full extent of his father's love for his hotel. Ten years after that, however, OG followed his mother Alice in suffering the amputation of a leg. For some time he had been finding it difficult to walk, and after the operation he was practically confined to Court Lodge, where special arrangements had been put in hand to ease his infirmities. In 1974 he died.

He had led a life rich in memories. He had toured the world as an enormously respected representative of his profession, and had welcomed through the doors of his hotel guests who were household names. Twice he had put the Goring at the disposal of his monarch, for in 1953, at the Coronation of Queen Elizabeth II, it had again become an annexe of the Palace. But the honour which gave him the greatest pleasure was being invited to make Prince Charles's christening cake in 1948. At a time of severe rationing, the Goring kitchens – supplemented by a Master Confectioner imported from Sheffield – produced a 75-pound work of art which it took four days to prepare. The ingredients, then impossible to buy in quantity, could not be supplied by OG alone but his friends in London's great hotels contributed handsomely. The finished cake was a triumph, and to this day a photograph of it occupies an appropriately prominent place in the hall of the hotel.

For sixty-four years the Goring had been the focus of Otto Gustave's life. For nearly fifty of them he had been actively engaged in its management and had overseen the changes, both structural and social, which had overtaken it. Under his stewardship it had become financially secure in a way given to few grand hotels of its, or any other era, but – and this is perhaps his most fitting epitaph – he had managed to do so, until perhaps the very last years of his life, without compromising any of the high standards which had been both his father's vision, and his legacy.

3 *The Chef's Tale*

The year was 1958. The *commis de rang* stood nervously in line. It was his first day at the Goring and the dining room was fully booked. At 12.30 the pace had been leisurely but now, half an hour later, an intimidatingly large crowd had arrived all at once. As usual, the staff coped admirably; Tony Perilli, the Head Waiter and a model of welcoming deference, seated them smoothly, produced menus with a flourish, and the station waiters began to hover expectantly. The *commis*'s own station waiter, loaded with dishes on his way to an already impatient table, had muttered an instruction at him as he passed and the young Englishman now found himself in the bedlam of the kitchen trying desperately to make sense of the orders being hurled at the chefs by the *aboyer* – the shouter – as he received the handwritten checks from those waiters at the head of the queue.

'Ça marche – deux lunch – deux smoked salmon – deux.'

'Oui.'

'À suivre. Un poisson du jour – un, et un roast beef – un.'

'Oui.'

'Deux pommes et légumes – deux.'

'Oui.'

The boy's nervousness increased as he looked down at the words he had scribbled on his pad. He moved slowly towards the hotplate, listening intently to those in front.

'Saucier – en vingt minutes quatre filets de sole bonne femme – quatre.'

'Oui.'

'Patissier – un flan aux cerises – un, un ice-cream armagnac et noisettes – un.'

'Oui.'

At last it was his turn. He handed his check over and the *aboyer*, barely glancing at it, shouted the words.

'Patissier – un plum pie – un . . .' His voice tailed off as he looked again, this time disbelievingly, at the piece of paper he was about to spike against the moment that the order would be fulfilled. The kitchen fell silent as the staff turned to look expectantly at Chef. They were not disappointed. Slowly the little Frenchman advanced, puce with rage, pausing only to pick up a heavy saucepan as he approached the quivering figure in the white apron.

'Plum pie? Qu'est-ce que c'est ce plum pie? Imbécile'. He waved his saucepan threateningly at the terrified *commis*. 'We do not 'ave plum pie. Fetch your waiter. Maintenant. Now. Go.'

At that moment the station waiter appeared, anxiously in search of both his assistant and the *pommes pailles* – the straw potatoes – that he had ordered so urgently but which had still, inexplicably, not appeared. He spoke quickly and soothingly to Chef who, with a final 'Bah!', turned on his heel and marched back in indignation to his stove. The situation saved, the kitchen returned to its usual condition of barely controlled commotion.

The professional lives of waiters and chefs are inextricably bound. Their relationship is rarely harmonious, often bad-tempered, and sometimes akin to civil war. Much depends on the personality of the two despots who rule in their respective fiefdoms – the Chef (there is only one Chef) and the Head Waiter. In this respect the Goring is perhaps luckier than many other first-class establishments, having enjoyed lengthy periods of tranquillity exemplified by the happy association forged in the early 1990s with the arrival of John Elliott and Richard Hand to take charge of the kitchen and dining room respectively – both being men of equable disposition, secure in the knowledge that they were at the top of their respective professions and had little to prove.

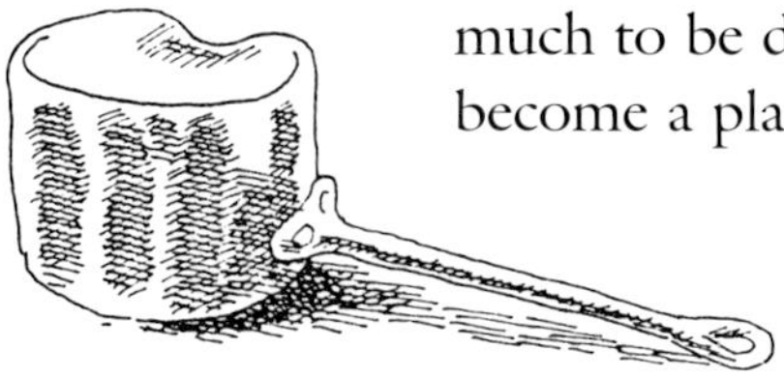

It was not always thus. In 1937 Paul Gasc had arrived, observing grimly as he unpacked his knives that there was much to be done if this most English of hotels was was to become a place fit for a Frenchman to eat in. Reluctantly, he admitted to himself that the ranges were first-class, and that the great iceboxes in which were stored the meat and fish – of excellent quality – were indeed adequate. But the dishes – 'Pouf!' – so English; so boring. As a *commis chef* at the Carlton at the turn of the century Gasc had been trained in the arts of both cooking and tyranny by the great Escoffier himself. Ten years at the Ritz as *saucier*, followed by spells as *sous-chef* at both Quaglino's and the Savoy, had honed his skills and brought him to the attention of OR Goring and his son who tempted him into their employment at a salary which never failed to make OG wince as he inspected his annual accounts over the next twenty-three years. In many respects Chef was a genius; his cooking skills were classically French while his inventiveness and gift for improvisation were to stand him in good stead during the years of rationing which were to be his lot for at least half his service at the Goring. He also had the necessary talent for *mise en place* – the putting into place – a term which describes the ability, essential in a top hotel chef, to manage the organization of a complicated empire made up of disparate departments – not only the sections (each headed by a *sous-chef*) dealing with sauces, roasts, vegetables, larder (cold foods), pastry, fish and butchery, but also those which produce private dining menus, breakfasts, room service, afternoon teas, and meals for up to 150 staff each day. Such a breadth of responsibility marks the difference between a first-rank hotel kitchen and even the very best of restaurants, whose chefs are positively pampered by comparison.

Paul Gasc was a traditionalist who ruled his domain with an unremitting discipline. His was, in every sense, the hot end of the kitchen. He fought an unrelenting battle with the waiters – to such an extent that they dreaded having to bring to him even the smallest complaint. Tony Perilli, the Head Waiter for much of Gasc's time, would shield his brigade from Chef's more intemperate revenges by schooling them to shift the burden to the customer. 'It's Lord Salisbury, Chef – I have a little note here from him saying that his chicken is a little undercooked. As for me, Chef, I can see clearly that it is perfect. But what can I do?' Even Gasc felt he could not pursue the noble Marquess through the dining room. In fact, he never appeared in the public rooms; the Goring had (and has) no flambé lamps or *guéridons*, the family feeling strongly that cooking should not take place at table where smells, however delicious, might intrude upon other guests.

In Gasc's kitchen, all walked in cautious awe – if not in actual fear. All, that is, but one. The exception was Wally Burley, a kitchen porter for nearly thirty years whose duties were to wash up the plates and operate the room-service lift to the floors above. Wally scorned the use of machines, dealing with over 1,500 plates a day by hand – some 13 million during his three decades at the Goring – and would never use the telephone to advise the floor waiters that their order was on its way, choosing instead to put his head into the lift-well and bawl at them – a procedure causing occasional consternation among those using the pavements above the kitchen windows. Classified

as unfit for service in the Second World War, Burley spent most of his time at the hotel, sleeping on the kitchen floor as frequent air raids prevented him from making the journey home. Throughout his years at the Goring he never had a day off for sickness, and was such a favourite of OG's that the General Manager, Norman Pennington, was put under the strictest of instructions: 'You can sack anyone – except Chef and Wally.'

If Burley's special relationship with the Goring family excused him from the worst effects of Gasc's tantrums, the rest of the kitchen staff were not so privileged. Edna Goring, entering incautiously one day, found herself facing the pastry *sous-chef* at a time when he was having the mother of all strips torn off him by Chef in full flow. The invective, as usual, was couched in a mixture of French and English, and in the course of the tirade the hapless victim's confectionery masterpiece was likened to ceiling plaster which should not be fed even to a dog for fear of invoking the RSPCA, while it was further suggested that he was better suited to a career in concrete mixing. Pausing to draw breath, Gasc was astounded to see the *sous-chef* winking at him – a desperate, albeit futile, attempt to convey to his tormentor that Madame Goring was present. Such insolence was not to be tolerated, and Gasc soared away into a detailed verbal examination of his minion's private parts, doubtful ancestry and lack of any future marriage prospects. No profanity was spared, no blasphemy unexplored. The pastrycook waited for another pause, before venturing a honeyed 'Can I help you, Madame?' Chef whirled round to find Edna – whose own power to make wrongdoers quail was scarcely less effective than his own – eying him grimly. He mumbled his apologies, stared down the amused staff until the smiles were wiped away, and promptly retired to his office for a glass of cognac.

Gasc's undoubted culinary talents were hardly given time to blossom before war broke out. A flush of patriotism overcame him and, packing up his knives, wife and children, he departed to Nancy to join the French Army. There, to his mortification, he discovered that age and family responsibilities disqualified him from military service. Judging, therefore, that England, being further from Germany, was likely to be a

more agreeable place in the foreseeable future, he headed back to the Goring. Wartime shortages and the subsequent extended rationing period brought out the best of his talent for improvisation. His five-shilling lunches became the talk of London. Every last and unlikely piece of scraggy black-market chicken was conjured with until it became something entirely delectable; his reputation for escalope of pork and for wiener schnitzel was so widespread that he attracted the attention of the authorities – until they discovered that the 'pork' (as also the 'veal') was in fact rabbit. He disguised the wholly disgusting whalemeat which he was forced by the regulations to endure, in a way which defied definition. Occasionally he had a windfall, as when, in 1942, an air marshal on leave delivered an antelope shot in the Western Desert, but for the most part, until the early fifties, he had to put up with the frustrations of working with raw materials deficient both in quantity and quality.

By 1960, however, his man-management techniques had become something of an anachronism. It was time for a change. Partly out of loyalty, and partly because Gasc's culinary skills, although a little dated, were undiminished, OG was reluctant to take the final decision. Luckily matters were eventually taken out of his hands when Gasc's son appeared unexpectedly, to announce that his invention of a small plastic tortoise with a nodding head had proved such a success in toyshops all over the world that he had made a fortune, and had therefore decided that his father should retire to a house in Provence where he could live out his life in the comfort befitting one who had given his working life to celebrating one of France's greatest traditions. After a suitably lavish and tearful farewell party, Chef left for the last time, spending his declining years eating in some of the best restaurants in France and, no doubt, giving their *patrons* the benefit of much free advice. M. Gasc *fils* continues to visit the Goring on his frequent business trips to London to stock the toyshops with an ever-increasing nodding menagerie.

Paul Gasc's successor, Arthur Gachet, had been the *saucier* and Deputy Chef for five years, but the decision to appoint him to replace the old tyrant was not an easy one. An anglicized Frenchman who spoke English with a cockney accent imbued in him by his London-born wife, he was an excellent cook, being particularly brilliant with fish. He was also both amiable and hard-working, qualities that persuaded Norman Pennington that the change of atmosphere which would certainly follow this move would outweigh any other consideration. OG was not wholly convinced but, uncharacteristically, gave way to his General Manager.

OG's doubts had centred on the fact that Gachet had never been a chef in his own right; his skills in *mise en place* had thus not been fully tested. He had never had to worry about gross-profit percentages or the intricacies of ordering; above all he had never experienced the responsibilities of planning the operation of the various departments. Had he the capacity for this sort of work? Was he, perhaps, too easygoing? There is little doubt that the kitchen staff revelled in the new, more liberal regime – sometimes with unfortunate results. *Sous-chef* O'Shea - always partial to a drop or more of the hard stuff but careful to conceal this predilection from Gasc and Pennington – soon learned to take advantage; one day George Goring found him asleep in Chef's office during a busy lunchtime with a daffodil behind his ear. The waiters too were happy; far from

dreading their appearances below stairs, they now positively looked forward to their exchanges with this most sunny of men, and the desirable harmony anticipated by the General Manager developed rapidly. But it was not enough. There was little discipline, and valuable management time was taken up in what should have been wholly unnecessary supervision.

Arthur Gachet's culinary abilities carried him through for ten years before changes in cooking techniques began to overtake him. Cuisine is as susceptible to fashion as women's clothes and the Chef found it difficult to adapt. He also lacked the ability to communicate an enthusiasm for the methods now in demand to the staff he was meant to be both tutoring and leading. In 1975, with mutual relief and without rancour, he and the Goring parted company, though he was often to return for staff celebrations and birthday parties – still exuding goodwill, and still popular with all those who remembered him.

The coming of Dieter Sondermann caused something of a stir in London hotel circles. He was Chef at the Westbury, then the flagship of the Forte hotel chain, and widely recognized as a rising star. George Goring laid his plans carefully, and when Sondermann responded to an invitation for a chat, the advantages of a move to the private hotel in Victoria were made clear. There was to be a generous increase in salary and, more important, it was emphasized that at the Goring it would be usual for management decisions to be forthcoming quickly – a situation which it is impossible to duplicate in hotels belonging to a large group, and an attractive working condition that has brought a number of key staff to the Goring. The chef took little time to make up his mind, departing from his previous post in a flurry of private and public recrimination directed at the Goring by both the general manager of the Westbury and the Forte hierarchy.

From the beginning, Sondermann showed himself to be a supremely competent organizer. He modernized – perhaps revolutionized is not too strong a word – the kitchens and displayed a welcome talent for administration which had been absent for far too long. Nevertheless, under his regime the Goring's cuisine never reached great heights, the cooking being characterized chiefly by a certain lack of adventure. A little like

Gachet before him, having settled into his ways – in Sondermann's case a preference for *nouvelle cuisine* – he found it oddly difficult to respond to new challenges. Even more unfortunately, he also lacked the drive necessary to motivate his staff first to attain, and then to reproduce the consistency of quality essential in winning the stars and rosettes which mark culinary achievement. But he, too, stayed for fifteen years – a reflection of the Goring's reluctance to part with faithful employees, and an example of a deep-rooted philosophy that loyalty, if it is to have any meaning, has to be seen to work both ways.

In employing John Elliott as Sondermann's successor from a field of applicants which included half the top chefs in London, George Goring took something of a risk. His doubts – not shared by general manager William Cowpe – centred on the fact that Elliott had only briefly been a *chef de cuisine* before he arrived for interview in 1990. Indeed his career pattern had been unusually varied, taking in a two-year spell with Ambassador Peter Jay at the British Embassy in Washington. His more regular credentials were impeccable. Numbered among his principal mentors had been Albert Roux who employed him at both Tante Claire and the Waterside Inn, and the great Michel Bourdin of the Connaught who was responsible for strongly recommending his protégé to the Goring. Bourdin had no doubt that John Elliott would find the elevation to Chef an effortless transition, and the move was trumpeted in both the trade and wider press.

At the beginning it seemed that Bourdin might have been wrong. The Goring's bright new star took some time to find his feet and come to terms with increased responsibility. Alerted by the publicity, restaurant critics were quick to sample the new man's work. Some came away disappointed. In particular Fay Maschler of the *Evening Standard* pointedly wondered how it was that Elliott's skills had impinged so little on, for example, the prominent hors d'oeuvre and dessert trolleys, not to mention other aspects of the menu such as an 'unforgivably badly made Cabinet Pudding'. It was the worst review of the Goring dining room ever published, and the owner, as well as most of the management team, was more than a little worried. But they had all – except Cowpe, underestimated their man. John Elliott was a quick learner; willing and intelligent, he soon acquired the necessary organizational skills and was able to turn his attention to induction training and the instilling of the all-important consistency into everyone from his senior *sous-chef* to the most recently joined *commis*, making each, however junior, understand that the standard by which they would be collectively judged would be that of the worst meal the kitchen produced. This led to a welcome acceptance of individual responsibility: a Chef can check the presentation of every dish, of every plate; what he cannot do is taste every product, and neither should this be necessary. Within eighteen months the gloom had lifted, and Bourdin had been triumphantly vindicated. George Goring was satisfied that, perhaps for the first time ever, he had one of the finest hotel restaurants in London.

One of Elliott's most estimable virtues is that he is eager to learn from others, quick to identify a talent and then exploit it to the Goring's advantage. To this end, he and his *sous-chefs* periodically swap places for a day or two with others in rival establishments, and, parties of eight are regularly taken from the kitchen to lunch or dine in London's greatest restaurants so that afterwards they can discuss the merits of the food they have eaten and see what lessons may be applied at their own stoves. Similarly, Elliott and Richard Hand, the Head Waiter, organize teams, composed equally of chefs and waiters, to eat after hours in the Goring dining room and experience for themselves life at the receiving end of their professions. Both the Chef and the Head Waiter are determined that their young staffs should understand the magic that can result when first-class cuisine is properly allied to superlative service, and they are encouraged to bring wives or partners to add to the enjoyment of these instructive occasions. It is, of course, the Head Waiter and his staff who bear the brunt – at least in public – of any lack of satisfaction expressed by guests. Such an incident is rare, and Hand, too, takes groups of waiters to dine elsewhere and observe the standards of others. No one, he feels, is too good to learn.

In the dining room, Richard Hand is in sole charge, his

responsibilities also stretching to the bar, the lounge and to room service; only the private dining rooms, run by the Deputy General Manager, are outside his control. His team of around twenty is split into two shifts, the first running from breakfast to luncheon and the second from luncheon to dinner. At 11 pm he hands over responsibility for room service and the bar to the Night Manager. Luncheon has always been the busiest of meals at the Goring and the two shifts merge to cope with the seventy-five or so covers, some of which will be occupied twice. Service is traditional, the Head Waiter, or his deputy, showing guests to their tables, producing the menus and seeing that all is comfortable. The station waiter, responsible for a number of tables, takes the orders and, assisted by his *commis*, delivers the handwritten checks to the kitchen, while the Head Wine Waiter sees to the drinks. Table waiters do not like dealing with drinks; their delivery interferes with the ceaseless flow between customer and kitchen and can be almost disastrously detrimental to the standard of service; similarly, demands from guests seated outside a particular station can also interrupt the smooth transition of food. Guests find this difficult to understand and are generally ignorant of the fact that apparently idle waiters are probably not idle at all but poised to swoop to the needs of their own allotted diners. At the Goring, the service is so effortless that guests are largely unaware of the demarcation.

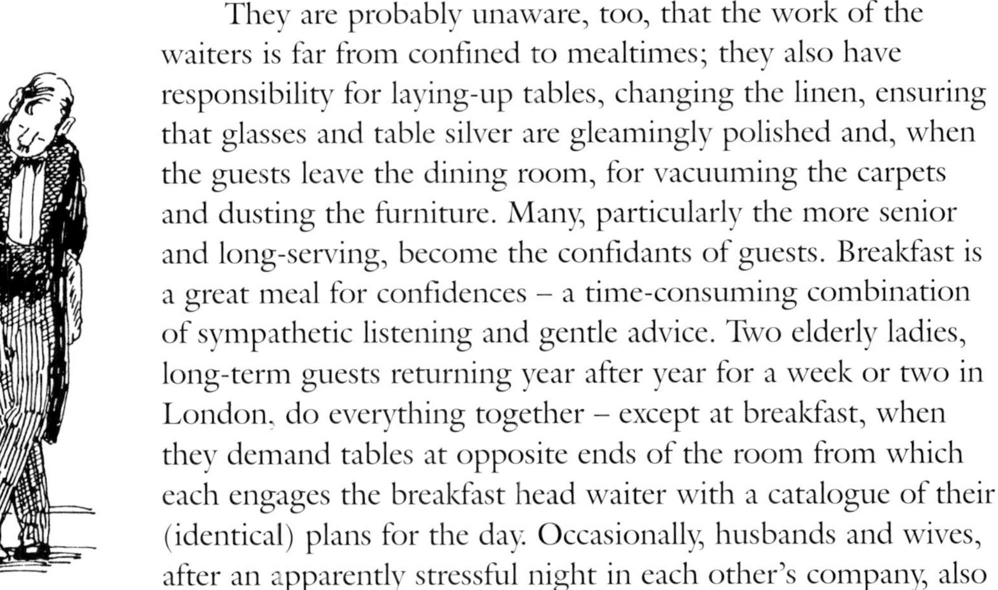

They are probably unaware, too, that the work of the waiters is far from confined to mealtimes; they also have responsibility for laying-up tables, changing the linen, ensuring that glasses and table silver are gleamingly polished and, when the guests leave the dining room, for vacuuming the carpets and dusting the furniture. Many, particularly the more senior and long-serving, become the confidants of guests. Breakfast is a great meal for confidences – a time-consuming combination of sympathetic listening and gentle advice. Two elderly ladies, long-term guests returning year after year for a week or two in London, do everything together – except at breakfast, when they demand tables at opposite ends of the room from which each engages the breakfast head waiter with a catalogue of their (identical) plans for the day. Occasionally, husbands and wives, after an apparently stressful night in each other's company, also want separate tables, or carry their differences into the dining room, appealing to their waiter to act as referee.

In the same way that regular customers of the Goring like to occupy the same bedroom at each visit, many insist on the same table. No. 8, a corner table for two, is particularly popular with a wide range of guests, including two demanding American ladies who, mercifully, have never yet stayed in the hotel at the same time (a recurring nightmare for Richard Hand); a Cambridge don known as the 'Mad Professor', and a Tory Cabinet Minister, often in for breakfast, who carries with him the additional complication of having to be kept away from two Labour MPs who are equally fussy about the company they keep. A titled lady who lunches in the bar once a week, and has been doing so for forty years, becomes so incensed if she finds her favourite table occupied that she is wont to telephone Edna Goring to complain.

There is, then, much juggling to be done, and more than a modicum of psychology to be applied, by the Head Waiter and his staff. Tact in abundance, together with a talent for never appearing to be discommoded (or even surprised), are essential qualities in dealing with the bizarre: for example the eccentric lady, rising eighty, who would always precede her lunch by downing four cherry brandies in the bar and who would then – scorning all offers of an arm – attempt to chart an uncertain course through the dining room to the table she always knew as her own. There is also the gentleman who treats his two nieces to dinner twice a month. Often the waiters notice that the nieces have changed radically in appearance, while sometimes he is so forgetful as to introduce them as his daughters. The ever-changing members of his string are bought wine considerably more expensive than that he offers to his wife, who is another one of his regular guests – but only at lunch.

From time to time incidents in the dining room have repercussions. On one occasion a cardinal archbishop, vast in girth and uncertain of temper – the personification of the Church Militant Here on Earth – was brought to dine by two priests. All was astonishingly reverential, the acolytes genuflecting so often and so deeply that the waiters were uncertain whether or not to bend down in unison. The

Cardinal, in the short intervals available to him when not engaged in eating with an all-consuming concentration and drinking more than a few glasses of wine of superior quality, spent the evening dismantling the vase of flowers in the centre of his table, petal by petal. When at last the party left, amidst more bending of the knee in which even the Deputy General Manager felt obliged to join, the *commis* clearing the table found a set of false teeth among the floral debris. The following morning the priests telephoned to inquire whether by any merciful chance . . . ? His Eminence was, it appeared, having a little trouble with his breakfast. One of them came round within minutes to retrieve the missing article, by which time the waiter, appalled at the condition of his find, had administered a thorough scrubbing and placed the now gleaming dentures on the concierge's desk for all to admire.

For all the expertise of its chefs and the care of the waiters, it is difficult for a hotel restaurant to reach the pinnacle of international culinary recognition. The standards of the *Guide Michelin* are absolute, and no allowance can be made in it for the complications which affect a kitchen fulfilling so many disparate calls on its time and expertise. Restaurants situated within some London hotels, for example Simply Nico's at the Grosvenor House and Marco Pierre White's operation at the Hyde Park, are franchise affairs serving only lunches and dinners and are not subject to the multifarious demands made of John Elliott and his team The ultimate has occasionally been achieved – at the Connaught for instance – but such exceptions are few. The Goring aspires to these heights and has, in the mid-nineties, come very close; it would surprise no one if this ambition – the top rating in *Michelin* – was fulfilled by the end of the century. Meanwhile chefs and waiters continue to do what they do best, responding – often pre-emptively – to the every whim of their guests. At that they excel; without fuss, without tantrum. An American lady, staying in London with her husband, the president of an international corporation, took her children to Paris while he was occupied on business. After two days the children wanted to go home. Home was the Goring – the food, they said, was better.

4 *The Porter's Tale*

The Union Internationale des Clefs d'Or is an organization with a *modus operandi* lying somewhere between that of Interpol and that of the Mafia. Membership, which is drawn from the concierges and head porters of grand hotels around the world, is by personal introduction, and the vetting procedures are rigorous. Its tentacles reach deep into airports, shipping lines, travel companies and ticket agencies – everywhere where personal contact can make a significant difference to the comfort and well-being of a favoured guest. Lost luggage is swiftly retrieved; unobtainable seats at sold-out performances are conjured up; airline seats are upgraded, and tables are booked at the most fashionable restaurants, even if they do happen to be on a different continent. Retribution can be equally comprehensive: a bounced cheque, a forged banknote or a stolen credit card will result in the description of the perpetrator being circulated to all members of the society – some seventy-five in London alone. Leslie Nicol – whose service at the Goring spanned forty-nine years – was telephoned by a fellow head porter in Scotland and told that a couple, posing as an earl and countess, had failed to pay their bill and were heading for London. Nicol put out their details on the Clefs d'Or network in the capital, eliciting an immediate response from the Hilton, which reported that a man answering the description had hired a Rolls-Royce through the hotel and failed to return it; a doorman had overheard the couple mention the Goring. The police were alerted and were lying in wait when the pair – he equipped with a deerstalker hat and exaggerated accent, she wrapped in an un-countess-like mink coat – arrived and tried to book a room. They were arrested and carted off to Rochester Row.

In 1933, Les Nicol, aged sixteen, short and slight of build, was sent by his local labour exchange to the Goring to be interviewed for the position of page boy. As he reached the hotel he noticed that the one other applicant had arrived before him. Told to wait by the Head Porter – 'And mind you keep out of sight of the guests' – he examined his appearance for the umpteenth time while his rival was sent in to be seen by Mr Gustave Goring. Soon it was young Les's turn; his references were examined, his family circumstances investigated. Finally, he was told to hold his hands out while OG walked slowly round him. Dismissed at last, his agony of apprehension was quickly at an end – the Head Porter told him he had the job; the other fellow had dirty fingernails!

Issued with his dark blue uniform, the tunic with a high-necked rose collar, complemented by black boots and white gloves, he joined the empire of William Bingham, Head Porter since before the Great War. A military looking man with fierce moustaches, Bingham controlled an extensive staff made up of not just his porters, the liftmen and three page boys, but also four valets – one to each of the bedroom floors –- and a team of male telephonists who manned the exchange. Nicol, examining his new clothes, was interested to see that the coat with its shiny brass buttons had a label on the inside inscribed with the word Tipper. Believing, no doubt correctly, that this was the name of the manufacturer, he sought confirmation from the valets. 'Oh no,' they said. 'Tipper was the name of the boy before you who was a great chap and bought us all pints of beer.' From that moment on he too would be known as Tipper – and expected to be just as generous.

Pages began work at 7.15 each morning, the young Nicol cycling in from his home in Mitcham. They would start by cleaning the brasses on the front doors, filling the inkpots, replenishing the writing paper in the public rooms, and carrying the silver ashtrays downstairs to be cleaned. Then came breakfast in the staff room before collecting the silver again and returning to take up their positions in the hall where, despite the gloves, their hands would be inspected by Bingham. For the next eight hours they would assist the porters, search for taxis, carry the bags, open doors and run the messages. It was a busy and happy life, albeit one structured even more severely than that in the military. Never did the otherwise ebullient Mr Goring, nor most certainly the taciturn Mr Gustave, speak to the lower orders except through their heads of department. The pages – at the bottom of this rigid chain of command – talked to no one senior to them unless spoken to first. Guests were addressed by their styles: 'Your Grace', 'My Lord' or, at the very least, 'Sir' and 'Madam'. To use an actual name by venturing, say, a 'Good morning, Mr Smith' was cause for complaint, and an inevitable thick ear for impudence from Mr Bingham. But there was always someone famous to goggle at and tips were plentiful, particularly for tasks undertaken outside the hotel: a telegraph taken to the Post Office, or a bet carried unobtrusively to a lurking (and illegal) bookie's runner, were always well rewarded, although the latter was severely frowned upon by an inappropriately named floor waiter called Virtue who had set himself up as the in-house bookie and much resented encroachment on his trade. Nicol's pay for the first year or two was 10 shillings a week, later reduced by a quarter when the *commis* waiters discovered that the page boys were being paid more than they were; Tipper, in common with most hotel staff at that time, relied on tips in order to live.

By the outbreak of war in 1939, he had been promoted to the telephone exchange, a post which carried some delicate responsibilities; all calls could be eavesdropped, and those to destinations abroad had to be booked in advance, their courses traced – exchange by exchange – as they crossed countries or continents. He had, however, little opportunity to garner any interesting titbits of gossip which this enviable position might have afforded him before, in company with almost all the men at the Goring other than the elderly or those classified as unfit, Tipper joined the Army. OG was then obliged to put up with a succession of temporary employees he was wont to describe as 'wasters and rotters kept up to any form of scratch only by the few remaining regulars'. It was the Goring's good fortune that among the non-combatants were William Bingham (because of his age), and Jock Grant, a valet with defective eyesight, who became Night Porter for the duration of hostilities, sharing OG's firewatching roster as well as manning the front desk during the blackout.

Between them, Bingham and Grant kept their department on the road, turning their hands to a variety of tasks not envisaged even in the Head Porter's most depressing peacetime nightmare. They and their ever-changing and dwindling staff not only coped with the duties prescribed for concierges, porters and doormen, but valeted, cleaned shoes, polished silver, swept floors, hung curtains, laid carpets and provided a room service to relieve the hard-pressed waiters. The long hours exhausted Bingham and, as the old staff began to reassemble in 1946, he retired, handing his post over to the returning Arthur Griffiths, who had been Night Porter before the war. Meanwhile, Tipper had also come home, having fought his way through North Africa and Italy with the 17th/21st Lancers, and was offered an interview at the Dorchester for the post of Deputy Porter. This would have meant promotion and, being now a family man, he went along to discuss terms with the manager, who told him that he would indeed be appointed but would have to hand over twenty-four clothing coupons for his uniform. This was not good news, so that when OG offered him the post of third porter and liftman at the Goring with the same wages as those offered by the Dorchester, but without having to part with any of his precious coupons, he accepted at some speed: £3 a week and about the same again from the porter's tronc (the pool into which waiters and other hotel workers pay their tips, and to which some managements contribute service charges, later shared out among the participants). Within weeks he was made assistant to Grffiths, and for the next twelve years they worked happily together until the latter's ill health forced him to retire.

Arthur Griffiths was a character. Apart from his military service, he had been at the Goring since 1929 and was well known to the hundreds of guests who now began to drift back to the hotel they knew so well. As Night Porter, he had had virtual carte blanche during the hours of darkness, and was a natural Mr Fixit in a way that would not have met with the entire approval of either OG or his father. Nothing was too much trouble for Arthur, but in his efforts to please guests he would often sail close to the wind, drawing the line only at turning a blind eye to any man who attempted to smuggle a woman past his ever-vigilant desk. In return, he made a small

fortune in tips, and where these were not forthcoming he took payment in kind – sometimes without permission. It is doubtful, for instance, whether the Earl of Moray, a resident for two years, was aware that Arthur often borrowed his town clothes while His Lordship was away slaughtering grouse in Scotland.

Among those also back from the war were Mersh Goodenough and Fred Scott, the fourth-floor valeting and luggage-service team who were to work together for over twenty years, occasionally trying their hands at other duties but always homing back to their favoured station, like pigeons to a loft. Like Arthur Griffiths, Mersh too had hidden depths not readily apparent to the management. For years he conducted a clandestine but mutually satisfactory affair with the Head Housekeeper, an arrangement seemingly about as unlikely as the Matron of St Thomas's Hospital having a liaison with a theatre porter.

The Goring was able to maintain its front-of-house staff levels for many years after the war's end, and doormen, luggage porters, valets, liftmen, and even two page boys, all remained in place. Travelling in the first postwar decade still kept the pace of a more leisurely age; air travel for the masses had not yet come into its own, and most of the hotel's overseas guests arrived at Victoria Station by train from Southampton, where they had disembarked from the great liners – Cunard for visitors from America, P&O for those from Australasia, and Union Castle from South Africa. The porters were kept busy collecting the enormous number of cabin trunks and other pieces of luggage which then accompanied even the most modest of travellers. Rationing made catering difficult, and Paul Gasc in his kitchen, improvising genius though he was, was hard pushed to please those for whom plenty was a way of life hardly interrupted by six years of war. American guests would often have cans of luxuries, unheard of in Britain, in their bags, which would be generously handed over to the kitchens or given to the staff as a tip. Les Nicol's part in alleviating the shortages was to be sent to Billingsgate Market in OG's car to collect boxes of fish. What the Goring could still provide in full measure, however, was a standard of personal service second to none. Teamwork was an essential element.

When Ted Powell – the hotel's painter and decorator for over twenty years – inadvertently knocked the hat of a lunchtime guest into one of his pots while touching-up the cloakroom, the Head Porter sent for his deputy. 'Don't just stand there, Tip, do something.' Nicol rang for the first-floor valet and between them and a liberal application of turpentine and soap, they had the hat back on its peg, clean, dry and brushed, before its owner came out to claim it. 'What a wonderful place, this is,' said the guest to his companion. 'Even over lunch, they brush your hat!'

What the guests appreciated above all was seeing the old familiar faces and being greeted and looked after as one of the family. In this the Head Porter and his team, together with the receptionists, played a vital role. It was they that a guest first encountered; they who made the all-important first impression on newcomers, and they – with the help of a comprehensive card-index system, later replaced by computer – who welcomed old-stagers as returning and personal friends. The Goring policy of promoting from within whenever possible paid off; occupancy rates rarely fell below 90 per cent even in the supposedly low season for London's grand hotels. This policy was exemplified again in 1958 at the time of Arthur Griffiths' enforced departure, when Tipper, now completing twenty-five years since he had first arrived, took his place, while Fred Scott, tiring finally of his partnership with Mersh, became Nicol's deputy.

Arthur Griffiths was a hard act to follow, but Tipper had for some time observed the need for minor changes in the department. Passenger aircraft were at last beginning to take the place of travel by sea, and this had a marked effect on the arrival and departure times of guests from overseas. No longer could they be relied upon to disembark at Southampton in the morning and arrive at Victoria an hour or so later. Often they would fly into Heathrow and be at the Goring for breakfast, overtaxing the relatively few night staff who did not go off duty until 9 am. Seeing the problem, Nicol recommended to OG that the day/night handover should be brought forward an hour at each end – a small step for mankind, perhaps, but not insignificant to a management disposed to regard most changes as a dangerous step on the slippery slope to hotel-chain conformity.

A more momentous alteration in employment conditions came about in 1964 when Tipper fell ill and had to go into hospital for three months. Never having been away sick before, he was slightly surprised on his return to work to find that he was to receive no pay for the time during which he had been laid up. OG explained to him that this was the practice at the Goring and that the rule applied to everyone, however long-serving. The senior staff, however, felt differently and demanded a meeting with OG and the General Manager, Norman Pennington – an unprecedented occurrence to which OG acceded only after considerable pressure from his son George, by that time working at the hotel as Pennington's assistant. There was a very public row between father and son during which it became clear to those present that young Mr George was a force to be reckoned with. The rules changed; a sickness benefit scheme was introduced, and the Head Porter was paid his three months' arrears in full. From that moment, the style of management was to undergo a subtle but unmistakable modernization.

Tipper Nicol ruled his front desk roost until 1982, finally retiring at the age of sixty-five. He is, in common with all the Goring's long-term staff, invited to the hotel's five-yearly celebrations. A decade and a half later, he continues to get Christmas cards from the guests he looked after over his forty-nine years, and gifts too from all over the world, including an annual Harrods hamper which has been arriving for more years than he cares to remember. At the retirement party given by George Goring, there were more than forty guests, including the entire Nicol and Goring families and past and present colleagues, as well as his great friend, Chesney Allen of the Crazy Gang, who had virtually made the hotel his home during a long run at the Victoria Palace.

Among the many others who are recipients of presents from grateful guests are Peter Sweeney and Fred Cashinas, the senior doormen and, as such, the very first of the Goring's staff to greet a guest. Sweeney, who has been at the hotel since 1965, was diagnosed as having cancer in the early 1980s, and was away for two years while the disease was treated. His job was kept open for him and his long months in hospital were eased not only by regular visits from management and staff, but from guests too. One prominent businessman, given to entertaining government ministers and captains of industry to lunch at the Goring, sent the doorman regular cheques when he learned the reason for his absence, and also found his son a job. Then, on Peter Sweeney's first day back on duty, he was astonished when a black car, complete with a police escort, came out of Victoria Square, and made a sudden and clearly unscheduled halt at the hotel steps. The passenger got out: 'Lovely to see you back, Peter,' said the Lord Chancellor.

While Sweeney's devotion to guests is by no means unique, he is prevailed upon more than most to give his services during his spare time. More than one American has persuaded him to drive them around the Cotswolds in his own car, while a Latin American lady will accept no hired chauffeur, or even a taxi, to take her shopping in the West End. It has to be Peter: 'When you meet me at the door, Peter, I know that I'm at home.'

It was Tipper Nicol who was responsible for recruiting a now long-serving but essentially unofficial member of the Goring team. John Shepherd had been driving a London cab for ten years when, quite by chance, he was waved down by the Head Porter, making a rare appearance on the pavement of Beeston Place. Nicol liked what he saw. 'Take this lady to Victoria Station,' he ordered. 'And then come back, if you please. I've got another job for you.' The 'job' was to Heathrow – in 1977 a cabman's dream, the £5 fare breaking the back of an average working day. Tipper and 'John Taxi', as the driver has been known to the hotel's staff ever since, became close friends, and soon Shepherd was on equally cheerful terms with the whole of the Head Porter's team. His relationship with the hotel was firmly cemented when George Goring's driving licence was 'borrowed' for three months – the magistrates taking the view that driving at 110 miles an hour during the rush hour on the M23 was overstepping the bounds of acceptability. John Taxi became his personal driver then and, when the occasion demands it, has remained so ever since. His work for guests of the Goring has enabled the cabman to confine his working life almost solely to the service of the hotel. A surprising number of visitors will accept no other driver, either in or out of the capital. Glyndebourne, Ascot, Wimbledon, and excursions to tourist attractions all over the country supplement regular runs to Heathrow as well as shopping, theatre and sightseeing trips within London itself. And he is a useful sounding board to the Goring, too, as he cautiously asks his passengers – particularly the first-timers – how they are enjoying their stay. It was, for instance, information supplied by the taxi driver which led to the televisions in each of the Goring bedrooms being lowered slightly to enhance the view.

John Shepherd has made many friends of his customers – particularly the Americans, with whom he has a particular affinity. He and his wife make regular trips to the United States to stay as guests of his fares. Josephine Barr – the Goring's sole American agent – employs him to drive her to far-flung corners of England to seek out other suitable hotels of the country-house variety which she might wish to add to her exclusive list. Occasionally she asks him to check a recommended hotel on his own – trusting that their long association has enabled him to know exactly her requirements. John Taxi, then, is imbued with the Goring concept of service, and subscribes to it naturally and wholeheartedly: 'This is a wonderful hotel,' he will say to all who will listen. 'It looks after the young and it looks after the old; everybody feels safe there, even ladies on their own. It may be known as the Boring Goring, but to me it's the best.' Not a lightly earned accolade from a naturally inclined socialist little given to the expression of flowery emotions.

The most recent in the distinguished line of Head Porters to grace the concierge's desk in the Goring's hall is Ernest de Blasi. Starting as luggage porter in 1975, he soon caught Tipper Nicol's eye as the man most likely to succeed him. His brief career in the industry had been one of escaping from the suffocating tentacles of the corporate image as first the Mayfair and then the Kensington Palace Hotels passed out of private ownership: 'I didn't know who my boss was any more.' At the Goring there was no doubt. Head Porter, General Manager and the owner himself all interviewed him, and it swiftly became clear that buck-passing had no part to play in that particular system of line management. His promotion to become Nicol's assistant was swift, and in 1982 he took full charge of the department.

By this time, manpower had been slimmed down. Page boys had gone and so had the valets, luggage porters now undertaking valeting duties. De Blasi, like his predecessors, rarely leaves his desk when he is on duty. It is his task to look after the guests from the minute they arrive until the moment they pay their bills and are ushered through the hotel doors to their waiting transport. In the time between, anything that is asked for by a guest, and which it is possible to obtain within hotel rules, is provided. To assist him he has two deputies, four luggage porters/valets, two doormen and three desk clerks. At night, when responsibility for room service passes to his department (from 11 pm to 7 am), there is a staff of six, supervised by a Night Manager. The day staff work shifts and Ernest himself is on duty from either 8 in the morning to 4.30 or from 11 until 8; the simple and satisfactory routine established by Les Nicol still holds good. When guests arrive, they are met by a doorman who takes immediate charge of their car and luggage. They are shown to the reception desk to book in and a receptionist, invariably female, collects the room key from the Head Porter and personally conducts the guests to their room, showing them round and making sure that they understand how to summon any form of help or seek any advice. Meanwhile the concierge desk has noted the details, and a luggage porter is dispatched by a separate lift to unite guest and bags within minutes.

Things do not always work as smoothly as de Blasi would wish, however. One day, a young couple with two small children arrived and insisted they had bookings. There were no empty rooms – not an unusual state of affairs at the Goring – and neither reception nor the concierge desk had any record of a reservation. Father began to shout the odds and children started to cry; not at all the sort of scene which a head porter would want to have taking place in full view of more orderly guests. The family was soothed, found a table in the lounge, and given cups of coffee and Coca-Colas. Father was asked if he had a confirmation slip, but a search of briefcase and baggage failed to unearth any such document. At this point Ernest had an idea and telephoned the Gore Hotel in Queen's Gate. Yes indeed, they carried the booking, and what was more, the family had been due to arrive the previous evening. The Head Porter broke the news gently. The man was disinclined to admit his mistake and demanded to speak to the Gore. 'Certainly, sir; no problem. Please follow me.' For three Christmases after this little fracas de Blasi received a handsome present from the eventually penitent family.

It would be difficult to exaggerate the influence that Ernest and his long-serving deputy, Tony Dabbenigno, exert on the reputation of the Goring, particularly among guests from the United States to whom de Blasi, in particular, is a legend. Neither man forgets a face or a name, and both set an impeccable example to the young receptionists and their team of porters. But no one is perfect, and there has been the occasional slip-up. A just-departed guest once telephoned from Heathrow to say that he had left a salmon in the hotel's deep-freeze. Could someone bring it down; the flight was due to leave for the States within the hour? Somehow – between kitchen and concierge – the message became transposed and when the porter arrived by taxi and told the hapless fisherman: 'I've come for the salmon you want us to keep for you, sir,' the American was hard put to it to remain equable. In short, he went berserk and the chastened porter returned both salmonless and without the tip he had been optimistically expecting. The Head Porter took full responsibility and began to explore ways of flying the fish to New York. He drew a blank – Federal Express refusing at that time to accept perishables – but by the time the guest had reached his home in New England, he found a Goring cheque waiting for him.

Some problems, however, are neither as straightforward nor as easily put right. The Goring has now come to terms with the fact that not all couples checking in are married, but it has an inflexible rule that guests booking a single room are not permitted to entertain a friend – of whatever sex – in that room. Neither does the hotel permit more than two people to retire to a double. This is not just a matter of moral judgement – fire regulations and insurance considerations play their part – but neither the Head Porter nor any member of his staff will knowingly comply with a request to be put in touch with a prostitute, either in or outside the hotel. 'Just walk up the road, sir, and look in any telephone kiosk,' is the most they will advise – together with a gentle admonition: 'And don't try to bring her back here.'

The Goring has always prided itself on the need to preserve strict confidentiality for its guests – however errant instances of individual behaviour might appear. It is the night staff who almost invariably bear the brunt of this issue, and extracts from the Night Porter's Report Book during Dennis Cooper's tenure of office in the 1980s are instructive. Names have been altered to protect the guilty.

> *Wednesday, 5th. 1130.* Room 42, Single Occupancy. Mr John Robinson seen to take a blonde 'Lady of the Night'

into the lift before I could stop him. After dealing with other guests, went up to the room and knocked on the door seven times without an answer. Contacted Mr Robinson by phone and informed him that his female must leave immediately. Female came down five minutes later.

Monday, 17th. 0130. Room 110, Single Occupancy. M. Le Brun (French national). Female arrived to see this gentleman and asked to visit his room. Refused. Guest informed and came down. They sat in the bar for ten minutes and then tried to make a break for the lift – in vain. Situation again explained to guest (I've had trouble with this one before) and both left the hotel together. 0700: M. Le Brun arrived back looking rather tired!

Monday, 3rd. 0100. Room 31. Single Occupancy. Sir William Toogood. Was informed that Sir William and two guests – one male and one female – had gone up to his room and ordered champagne. Contacted Sir William to ask whether guests were staying at the hotel and informed that they were not. Told him that we could not serve drinks to his friends unless they came downstairs. Male person came down, saying he could not find the female. He then left. Went up to Room 31; no sign of female so instituted a search and found her in the fourth-floor linen cupboard! Escorted her from hotel. She was very tanked up with drink.

Thursday, 22nd. 0300. Room 73. Mr Richard Minsky (US national) rang down to ask me to fix him up with a Linda Lovelace type female. Explained to guest that we were a No-Go Area in this respect. Suggested we sent him up a do-it-yourself kit (a *Playboy* magazine and an empty Marmite bottle). Guest refused offer but I think he got the message.

Occasionally the more usual roles are reversed.

Friday, 9th. 0510. Stopped young male bearded and bejeaned person (who had come down the stairs) from leaving the hotel and inquired who he was. He informed me that he was not a guest but had been staying with Mrs S Mackinson in Room 45. Checked this out before I let him depart. (Mrs Mackinson sounded very sleepy – not surprised, he looked a big lad!). She is paying double rate. Lucky old her.

Friday 14th. 0310. Miss Valda Kuhlmann (US national, Room 102) came back into the hotel and insisted on speaking to Michael and Andrew, my night porters. I asked the boys what she wanted with them and they informed me that she wanted them both in her room!!! It would appear that she's been trying to have them all week. It never happens to me.

Michael and Andrew were clearly personable young men. Quite soon they were in further demand.

Wednesday 16th. 0240. Mr Chumleigh. Room 44. Michael informed me that Mr Chumleigh had come back into the

> hotel and kept winking at him and giving him the glad eye. Guest rang down for Perrier water and asked for Michael to deliver it. Sent Andrew up instead and he came back VERY FLUSHED. Guest had nothing on and requested Andrew to come into his room. Andrew fled. Mr Chumleigh again telephoned and asked to book a morning call and pleaded 'Please come . . . please come . . . please come.' All three of us locked ourselves in the breakfast room!

Illicit sex is not the only problem, although other incidents tend to be even rarer.

> *Tuesday, 12th. 0620.* Black female appeared from luggage lift. Can't think how she got upstairs, none of us saw her – perhaps during the day? She had a large bag and when I asked to see inside, she dropped it and ran out of the hotel like the clappers! Bag contained two towels, two pillow slips, two single bed sheets and a face cloth. No doubt she had spent the night with a guest. I don't know who but Mr Rogerson (Room 64) booked an early call at 06.00 and he still had not appeared by 8. Have informed morning housekeeper of contents of the bag. We shall see.

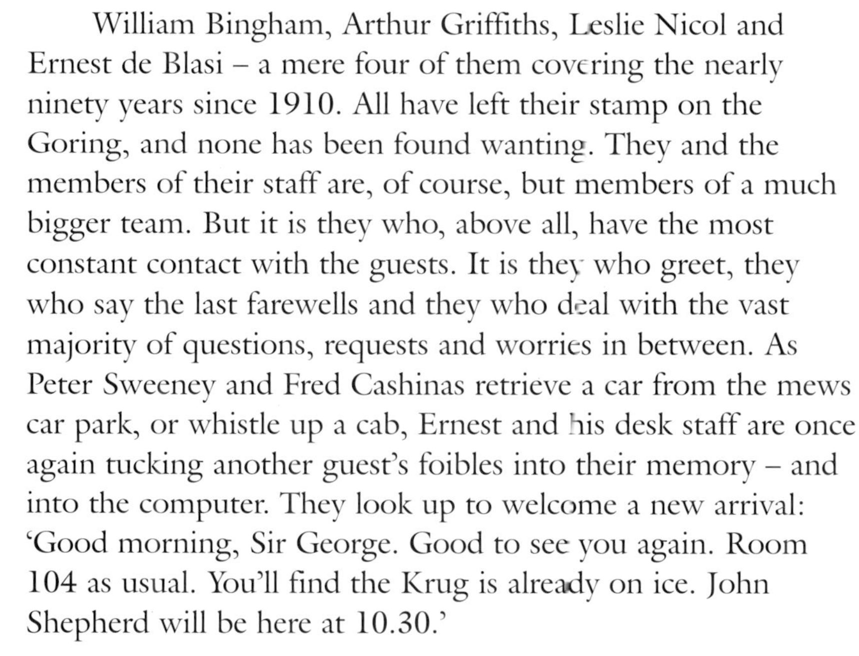

William Bingham, Arthur Griffiths, Leslie Nicol and Ernest de Blasi – a mere four of them covering the nearly ninety years since 1910. All have left their stamp on the Goring, and none has been found wanting. They and the members of their staff are, of course, but members of a much bigger team. But it is they who, above all, have the most constant contact with the guests. It is they who greet, they who say the last farewells and they who deal with the vast majority of questions, requests and worries in between. As Peter Sweeney and Fred Cashinas retrieve a car from the mews car park, or whistle up a cab, Ernest and his desk staff are once again tucking another guest's foibles into their memory – and into the computer. They look up to welcome a new arrival: 'Good morning, Sir George. Good to see you again. Room 104 as usual. You'll find the Krug is already on ice. John Shepherd will be here at 10.30.'

5 *The Distaff Tale*

Maria was fed up. Or rather, she reflected gloomily as she contemplated the mish-mash of undercooked chicken and overboiled cabbage that constituted her lunch, she was hardly being fed at all. If this was how English hotels expected their staff to eat, she would be better off at home in Munich. 'MauMau pie' was what the other chambermaids called it, but the allusion to the supposed eating habits of African guerrillas in some far off British colonial war was as imperfectly understood by Maria as was the reason for this daily assault on her digestive system. It was not that she didn't enjoy her work; she had now been at the Goring for over a year and Mrs Schoeffter, the Head Housekeeper, was strict but fair, looking after her team of chambermaids, cleaners and seamstresses with the vigilance of a mother hen. But even she seemed unable to take up successfully the constant complaints about the food in the staff dining room. She had, she said, spoken with Mr Pennington, the General Manager, and even been to see Monsieur Gasc in his kitchen – an encounter from which the Housekeeper had been observed to retire to her sitting room for a restorative glass of cherry brandy – but all was apparently to no avail: MauMau pie or its equally disgusting variations continued to constitute the staple diet. Maria's Bavarian blood boiled as she pushed the unappetizing mess around her plate. She came to a decision. Abruptly gathering up her tray, she marched purposefully out of the room. She, herself, would talk to Mr Goring.

Unknown to the chambermaid, OG had left his office for the rest of the day. He had to attend one of the many lunchtime engagements which, by 1965, were increasingly taking up much of his time. Before leaving he had given his son – newly arrived and installed as an assistant manager – an important assignment. He was to sweet-talk the recently ennobled chairman of a national company and persuade him that the Goring was just the place at which to put up his more important clients from abroad. He was then to give His Lordship luncheon. Young Mr George was at his most expansively persuasive as he listed the Goring's charms: the rooms were probably the most comfortable in London; Chef was at the top of his considerable form and, above all, the staff were the most polite, the most caring, the most deferential. None surpassed them. The chairman was impressed. George relaxed; it was in the bag.

In upon these delicate negotiations burst Maria, quivering with indignation, tray firmly clutched in both hands. She slammed her burden down on the leather topped desk, noticing too late that the target of her wrath was, unexpectedly, the (she had observed with some interest) rather *schön* Goring son, and not the cantankerous old man she had been expecting. The smile on George's face became fixed as he inspected the unappetizing contents of the plate. 'Ah Maria,' he said. 'Don't tell me that this is your lunch?' The chambermaid collected herself; in for a pfennig, in for a mark: 'No, Mister George. This is not my lunch – this mess is now your lunch.' With a final triumphant 'Huh!' she swept out, scattering the scandalized secretaries in the Manager's office. A bemused Norman Pennington reached for his telephone. He must tell the Housekeeper to sack the girl immediately.

In the inner sanctum, the well-luncheoned chairman looked interestedly first at the food and then at his host. Something appeared to be amusing him. His lips twitched. 'Well,' he said. 'What are you going to do about that?' 'What I am going to do,' said George, 'Is put her in charge of staff food.'

The part played by women in the successful operation of the Goring has been important, often crucial. Two departments, those of housekeeping and reception, have always been largely female domains, while the personal secretaries and the successive Mrs Gorings have invariably exercised a powerful influence, something well recognized by senior staff and the more perceptive of regular guests.

Receptionists have a key part to play in fulfilling a first-time guest's expectations. It is a receptionist who takes charge once the doorman has performed the initial civilities. Confirming personal details and collecting the room key from the concierge, she escorts her charges to their room, pointing out the geography of the hotel and describing the services the Goring provides. Having arrived at a bedroom and while awaiting the arrival of the porter, she explains the operation of lights, telephone, television and the other appliances. When guests and luggage are reunited she withdraws, finally reminding her charges that if anything else is needed, all they have to do is pick up the telephone. Those who have stayed at the hotel before – however long ago or infrequently – are greeted by name and will find that any personal preference has already been catered for: an ice bucket filled, extra pillows on the bed, a bottle of malt whisky on the table. Occasionally, even in the early days, customers would be surprised to be confronted with such detailed knowledge of their personal habits. In 1912, the Head Receptionist was Miss Jarvis, an Irish Catholic martinet who initiated the card-index system on which were recorded guests' individual foibles. An unwilling witness in a case of alleged adultery, she was subpoenaed by the Divorce Court to give evidence of occupancy of a room. Miss Jarvis did not approve of divorce, and her impatience with such an ungodly procedure extended to those who administered the law. The judge questioned her closely. Was Room 57 a double room? Was it furnished with two single or one double bed? To the witness, such questions were a waste of her valuable time. She wanted to be back behind her desk. 'You ought to know, My Lord,' she snapped. 'You've slept there often enough.'

The qualities needed by a successful receptionist extend far beyond the possession of an attractive appearance and a friendly, communicative nature. Intelligence and a high level of numeracy are necessary: it is receptionists who make up and present bills, receive payment and deal with foreign currency exchanges; each, when coming on shift, receives a personal float, and thousands of pounds pass daily through their hands. Until the 1970s they made up bills by hand using their own fountain pens, accounting for scribbled receipts from bar, dining room and room service on tabular account sheets, a laborious procedure demanding careful attention to detail as well as scrupulous honesty. Sweda machines – a sort of superior cash-register – were then introduced, and these were replaced in turn by the hotel's comprehensive computer system which, in 1991, finally did away with the last vestiges of handwritten bookings and personal cards. The disappearance of the manual telephone exchange – a male preserve so beloved of both OR Goring and his son – added telephone duties to the receptionists' remit, although this, mercifully, has never led to the irritatingly chanted: 'Goring-Hotel-Janice-speaking-how-may-I-help-you?' school of answering favoured by most hotel chains. A plain, unsung 'Good afternoon; Goring Hotel' is the prompt and economical response to an outside call.

Young, intelligent and presentable females do not always find shiftwork congenial and the turnover of receptionists is, at least by the standards of Goring staff, unusually high. Belinda Svensson, for example, came to the hotel in 1990 as a junior for only a year before becoming a shift-leader starting work at either 8 in the morning or 3 in the afternoon. Married and ambitious to progress in hotel management, she could discern no immediate opening for further promotion at the Goring and so left after five years to join her husband outside the industry while considering her longer-term future. There are other difficulties, too; not the least of them being that the girls are occasionally propositioned. Particularly persistent in modern times is the still relatively rare Russian businessman who, perhaps as a result of his new-found freedom to travel in the West, finds it difficult to accept that the friendly young lady showing him to his room is not throwing in her body as part of the service. Some Japanese guests, more obliquely,

enquire diffidently whether it might be possible to buy a 'spare pillow', and unaccompanied males of all nationalities are wont to ask for a massage. This the receptionist will always arrange, explaining gently that a masseur will be summoned – a response almost invariably followed by an embarrassed silence and a sudden change of heart.

An exception to the quick turnover was Thelma Fabian who arrived as Head Receptionist in 1955 and stayed for twenty-five years. Trained for the ballet, an illness forced her to take work in her aunt's small hotel in the country, from which she graduated to the Green Park in London. OG's promise of promotion lured her to the Goring, although at first he offered £5.10s a week – rather less than she was getting at the Green Park. Supported by Pennington, she held out for £6, then accepted the job and joined four other girls in residence at No. 10 Victoria Square, where she assumed a role not unlike that of the senior prefect in a school dormitory. Immediately she felt at home: 'It was like joining a happy family.' True, the head of that family was rather distant and aloof, but Norman Pennington was kind and gentle, and she soon made close friendships among other members of the senior staff, notably Tipper Nicol, Edwina Davy (OG's personal assistant) and Mary Scoggins, Pennington's own secretary.

Thelma Fabian arrived at a time when the Goring was beginning, almost imperceptibly, to trade rather too complacently on its past glories. OG's slowly failing health, his outside commitments and reluctance to spend money, left little time for any serious consideration of how his hotel might best adapt to a fast-changing world. Heavy personal taxation and the ever-increasing burden of death duties were beginning to dissipate the disposable incomes of its traditional British clientele. Sons and daughters of the gentry, keen to come to grips with the exciting social challenges of the 'Swinging Sixties', found the Goring too staid and moved into shared flats; the long-established extended bookings for the Season evaporated (as, effectively, had the Season itself when, in the 1950s, debutantes ceased to be presented at Court). It wasn't that standards fell – guests continued to be cosseted as they always had been, being encouraged to feel as if they were staying in a private house with a particularly solicitous staff – it was just that, in the prevailing national mood to modernize, the hotel was being left a little behind. Occupancy rates remained high, largely because of the growing ease of transatlantic travel and the desire of a certain class of American visitor to be transported out of a hectic world into a more gracious age, but the now slightly old-fashioned furnishings, and an absence of up-to-date technological equipment, were becoming apparent. There was in short, a lack of will to move with the times.

All this was of little concern to Thelma Fabian and her receptionists as they continued to make friends of their guests while calming down the occasional over-demanding crosspatch. Each girl had her favourites among the guests, and some fell in love, causing much covert amusement among the others as the starry-eyed one strove to maintain a proper on-duty formality with her lover. Thelma, too, had her share of admirers, but drew the line at any of her girls entertaining their young men in No. 10. In this, her direction to them was admirably succinct: 'If I can go elsewhere to get my nookie, then so can you. We can't have the other residents in the square thinking we're running a brothel!'

If Thelma, as Head Receptionist, saw herself as protector of the Goring's good name, the undisputed guardian of the guests' comfort has always been the Housekeeper, a post as important in its sphere as that of the Chef in his. One of OR's favourite homilies neatly summed up her duties: 'We make a profit while our guests sleep, so see that they sleep in peace.' Successful housekeepers are more likely to be born than made, and the department has traditionally been a female preserve although OG did his bit to break that particular mould by writing the standard handbook on the subject. His theme in essence was that 'while hotel cooking is not domestic cooking magnified, hotel housekeeping is certainly housewifery on a larger scale.' He went on to recommend that an ideal candidate for the post would have acquired a full range of hotel experience before becoming a specialist and fitting herself for final promotion. So it was with Mary Davin. Coming to the Goring in 1975 as an assistant housekeeper to the effervescent 'Attie' Atwell, and after a grounding in one of the grandest of London's hotels, this quietly spoken, supremely competent

Irishwoman soon graduated to the top position, which by 1995 – the year in which, sadly, she was forced to retire through ill-health – carried with it responsibility for a staff of thirty, including two deputies. She, like her predecessors, was directly answerable to the General Manager for the cleanliness and basic maintenance of the interior of the hotel, the administration of the linen (through a head linenkeeper), the staff accommodation and, most importantly, the security of the bedrooms.

Sharing shiftwork with her deputy, Mary's day began at 7 with the supervision of the general cleaners. Collecting a list of departing and incoming guests she would then brief her dozen or so chambermaids (or 'room attendants', as they have become known in deference to male infiltration) so that the appropriate rooms could be properly prepared. Occupied rooms are treated individually, the cleaning and linen changing being carried out in guests' absence – chambermaids introducing themselves to new arrivals as soon as possible in order to make the necessary arrangements. During the afternoon the Housekeeper inspects every one of the hundred rooms, checking on the work of her subordinates. The standard of bedmaking, the cleanliness of carpets, upholstery, basins, baths, lavatories and the replenishment of toiletry baskets all come under the minutest of scrutiny. Small deficiencies are noted: a burnt-out lightbulb, a suddenly squeaky bed (some take a lot of punishment), a dripping tap, a loose screw. Nothing must be overlooked. If a guest has to ask for a fault be rectified, the Housekeeper has demonstrably failed.

The very first Housekeeper at the Goring was Alice, OR's wife, who set the standards which led to the hotel being recognized as one of the best-kept in London. Her assistant, Miss Smith, succeeded her at the outbreak of the First World War but was snapped up by Claridge's when the Goring was taken over by General Pershing. For some years after 1918, staff of the highest calibre were hard to come by, and housekeepers came and went until the arrival of the loyal and hard-working Miss Wilkins in 1924. She remained at her post until 1946, being then well over seventy but having seen both OG and the Goring through the Second World War despite being frightened almost witless by the bombing. There followed a number of what OG described as 'shockers' including one lady who thought she discerned an opportunity to supplement her wages by procuring the chambermaids to service male guests in a way not envisaged by the *Housekeeper's Handbook*. She had picked the wrong hotel for this sort of entrepreneurial activity, and was sacked overnight.

The Goring's good name – and the equilibrium of its Managing Director – was restored by the estimable Mrs Hersee, a gentle Indian widow whose husband had successfully operated the best hotel in Basra (Iraq, at the head of the Persian Gulf), who rejuvenated the personal record cards which had been sadly neglected since Miss Wilkins's departure. Mrs Hersee stayed for seven years and was followed by the formidable Mrs Schoeffter, for two years the deputy and, despite her Belgian married name, an Englishwoman. An exception to OG's own guidelines, Mrs Schoeffter knew nothing of the hotel business when she arrived at the Goring but had made an outstanding impression at her interview, giving OG to understand that she was an expert seamstress and would be willing to put this expertise at his disposal. This she did, removing the need for expensive outside refurbishing work on curtains and furniture fabric – a cost-cutting exercise dear to the proprietor's heart. Like her predecessors – and, indeed her successors – Mrs Schoeffter took her moral responsibilities towards her largely female team seriously. She came quickly to the rescue when a regular guest, an elderly man, ostensibly confined to a wheelchair, took to summoning his chambermaid late in the evening and greeting her while levering himself upright, stark naked and in a state of advanced sexual excitement. 'Ready for action he is, Mrs Schoeffter, and at his age too!' The Housekeeper sailed into action. Responding to the nightly call in person, arms akimbo and black skirts rustling with indignation, she told the old gentleman that in future his bell would be answered by a male valet of undoubtedly heterosexual inclination who might well consider such an exhibition a slur on his manhood. Here Mrs Schoeffter was on sure ground – the valet she had in mind was the long-serving Mersh Goodenough with whom she was conducting a clandestine affair which she fondly imagined was a secret. In fact the liaison was a favourite topic of gleeful gossip among the senior staff, as well as enlivening the day of the

whole corps of chambermaids. It was something of a minor miracle that neither OG nor the somewhat puritanical Norman Pennington ever came to hear of it.

Of the innumerable women who have served the Goring loyally since its inception, none have had a greater impact or acquired such an intimate insight into its management as Edwina Davy and Mary Scoggins. From 1952 until 1984, Davy (no one ever used her first name) was the personal Assistant, first to OG, and then to George Goring, while Mary, who arrived in 1955 and stayed for thirty years, was the hotel's senior secretary, being responsible to Norman Pennington until his death in 1970, and then to William Cowpe. Together with Thelma Fabian, with whom they shared lodgings, each in her own way contributed much to the worldwide reputation of the Goring.

Davy arrived from a country hotel in Lincolnshire and immediately felt in sympathy with the contented atmosphere prevailing among the senior staff. About her new employer she was not so sure. His demanding reputation was well known, and she was not at all reassured by being told that if she lasted six months she would be perfectly equipped to name her own terms at any hotel in the land. She felt, moreover, that she had already got off on the wrong foot by refusing to start immediately, insisting to OG that she be allowed to work out a proper notice with her old employer. In the beginning she found the decidedly upstairs-downstairs regime at the Goring difficult to come to terms with, but her sense of humour was so infectious that even her aloof employer found it difficult to keep his distance. Soon she had him laughing at himself in a way he rarely displayed and which, to his surprise, he found rather agreeable. But even so, any feeling of cosy intimacy was confined strictly to the office. When accompanying OG to an outside business meeting, Davy would invariably be put in a taxi to travel separately, OG considering it unacceptably improper to arrive at a meeting sharing a car with his secretary. Strangely, he never made his reasons for this singular behaviour plain, always finding a transparently obscure excuse at the last minute to send her on ahead. This curious reluctance to face squarely up to his own convictions manifested itself in a number of other minor ways. Some months after taking up her post Davy was engaged in typing a letter which OG had dictated before leaving the office on outside business. Edna Goring arrived on her way to a shopping expedition, talked a little and then asked to see what Davy was doing. She looked at the letter and frowned.

'That won't do at all,' she said. 'Now listen, and I'll tell you what to say.'

The wording adjusted to her satisfaction, Edna went off to the West End. With some misgiving, the PA began again and had just finished when OG returned to sign it off. Davy explained the changes; her employer was enraged.

'You work for me. Please write the letter I dictated. You do not work for Mrs Goring.'

Patiently, Davy put in another sheet of paper. OG watched her as she tapped away. Edna returned, laden with packages and, after greeting her husband briefly, she turned to the desk.

'Have you done the letter, Miss Davy?'

'I have done *a* letter, Mrs Goring. Mr Goring said that I was to do the letter he gave to me.'

OG shuffled his feet as Edna glared at him

'I'm sorry, darling,' he said. 'I never said that to Miss Davy. She must have misunderstood.'

From that moment, Davy got a clear message and where there was a conflict, always obeyed Edna – no matter how contradictory to OG's orders his wife's wishes might be. In matters of marital disagreement, there was no doubt who had the final say. Even given that she got on, personally, very well with the redoubtable Mrs Goring – Edna had from the start made her very welcome – Davy recognized that if she ever quarrelled with her, she might as well pack her bags the same day.

Like others who knew the Goring family well, Edwina Davy came to understand that OG's failings stemmed in part from his uneasy relationship with his father, and from the fact that in some respects Edna had assumed OF's mantle. Both – albeit with the best of intentions – tried to make of him something which he was not. Shy, reserved and essentially unassuming, OG was just not up to playing either the genial host or taking up a high-profile place in the limelight of international hotel circles. He preferred to work behind the scenes, finding it agony to engage in gentlemanly banter with his guests, or to manoeuvre his way on to the top tables of professional gatherings. He knew where his strengths lay: he ran one of the best hotels in London, he made a great deal of money for his family, and he had his writing, through which he enjoyed communicating his wealth of knowledge and experience to those finding their way in the profession. He wanted nothing more from life and, even at his country home, he found it difficult to play the flamboyant squire in the way relished by his father – preferring instead to produce exquisite little tapestries and entertain quietly at the dinner table. He was also the product of a deep-seated – almost Prussian – tradition of adherence to a fixed and immutable social order to which he stubbornly clung even in the fast-moving times through which he lived in his later years. This failure to adapt was perhaps the greatest single cause of the almost impenetrable stockade of aloofness with which he surrounded himself.

Davy, together with other senior staff at the Goring, saw this agony clearly, readily forgiving him his obstinacy and understanding that his studied condescension towards them sprang from an ingrained uncertainty when forced to confront personal relationships. They respected him for his single-mindedness – a man resolutely pursuing, in the only way he knew, the prosperity of his hotel and the happiness of its guests. This shared understanding united them into a close-knit community for whom the well-being of the Goring also became their own primary – in some cases, their only – concern. They watched too the efforts that Edna made to protect her husband in his illnesses, and the way she ensured that he was never, even near the end of his life, made to feel that he was anything but in sole charge. And, on the whole, they approved.

Scoggs – Mary Scoggins – saw matters from a different perspective. Whereas Davy ran OG's personal and professional life, dealing only peripherally with matters concerned with the internal running of the Goring, Scoggs's work as secretary to successive General Managers gave her a comprehensive knowledge of the hotel's administration, and an intimate insight into the lives of the staff and not a few of the guests. It was with Scoggs, for example, that a distraught Sarah Churchill, daughter of Sir Winston, sought refuge one sad day when she was being pursued by the police following a drunk and disorderly offence in Beeston Place. Like Davy, on her arrival Mary immediately became aware that she had joined something special – everyone seemed so proud of the Goring and their own role within it. Norman Pennington was patient and helpful, while OG treated her (then aged thirty) as a little girl who had come to a new school. Sensitive to atmosphere, she soon came to understand that although the proprietor and General Manager had worked together for nearly twenty years, they were by no means close friends. It was apparent that OG saw Pennington as just another employee – highly valued, deeply trusted, and, of course, the most senior – but an employee none the less and one who, despite his position, would never dare to say even 'Good morning' until OG had spoken first. They never, as far as Scoggs was aware, had a difference of opinion over policy, Pennington always deferring with hardly a demur.

Mary dealt with all the hotel's correspondence except that addressed to OG personally and was impressed to find hardly a letter of complaint. There were, however, many of praise, the contents of which Pennington made sure were passed to the appropriate staff. She was highly diverted by an instruction that she was to save every used envelope – OG insisting that they should be retained and re-used for the weekly staff wages.

The stamps, too, were carefully removed and passed to OG, though their eventual destination remained a matter of constant speculation among the office staff. OG's drinking, and the care he took to conceal it, also gave much innocent pleasure, particularly as his sometimes erratic behaviour in public meant that he was not always as successful as he might have wished. There was, for example, the occasion when he called a taxi, the door of which as always was held open for him by the senior doorman. The latter was considerably surprised when OG – thinking perhaps that he had arrived at his destination – stopped the cab after it had gone only ten yards and got out on the far side, giving the hapless doorman a severe ticking-off for not opening the offside door and seeing the proprietor safely back on to the pavement!

Mary Scoggins was the first provider of secretarial assistance to guests – later a regular and highly technical facet of the Goring service. In the late 1950s, in response to this new demand on her services, Scoggs would go to a client's room after normal office hours to take dictation. One such assignment led to what was to prove to be a twenty-five-year love affair. Fearing that discovery would mean instant dismissal, she managed to conceal the matter from the senior management. Her friends, however, soon discovered the arrangement and entered into the conspiracy with a will. Being careful not to break either the hotel rules or those laid down by Thelma Fabian for conduct at No. 10, the lovers had to make alternative (and expensive) provision for their more intimate moments. 'I bet I've been booked,' she once declared, 'into more London hotels than most Conservative MPs!' The staff, particularly the doormen, all became used to her arriving for work in her little car after such assignments, but Graham Woolcott, an assistant manager, was surprised to find Mary and her lover checking into an hotel in Eastbourne one Friday evening. He had only said goodnight to her a couple of hours earlier as they both left the Goring exchanging best wishes for a restful weekend at home!

Thelma Fabian, Edwina Davy and Mary Scoggins deserved in full the honours paid to them on their retirements – the parties, presents and pensions were just and well-earned rewards. For nine decades they and a whole host of women have done much to enhance the Goring's reputation. All have been free agents, mistresses of their own lives – able to come and go as they pleased or saw fit, bound only by personal loyalty and a contract of employment. But for three others who played crucial, if widely dissimilar, roles in the hotel's history, the ties have been less elastic. These are the Goring wives.

The tiny, elegant Alice set the pace. Not only was she the first of a distinguished line of Housekeepers, she guided her essentially foreign husband through the intricacies of the English social scene, supplementing OR's shrewd hotelier's instinct with precise definitions of the standards that would be required to please a distinguished (and monied) county clientele. Her part in insisting that her son should go to a public school ensured that OG, too, would acquire an appreciation of the needs of the gentry, and her wholehearted acceptance of her daughter-in-law made for a smooth transition when the time came for Edna to take her part in the hotel's business.

Edna, beautifully dressed and expensively educated at home and abroad, although distancing herself from the Goring while she brought up her family, was able to contribute a first-hand knowledge of the requirements of big business, a world in which she had been immersed by her father at an early age. An enthusiastic traveller, she encouraged OG to play a full part within the international hotel trade, as well as seeing that his solid contributions to the industry in the United Kingdom were recognized for their considerable worth. Perhaps even more importantly, she was able to support her husband when he needed help most, providing him with a comfortable country retreat and even turning that into a practical supplier of much-needed garden produce for the Goring in times of scarcity. As she came to play a more active part in the management of the hotel, dealing with those areas which OG's preoccupations and illnesses had led him to neglect, she made a considerable mark, insisting on regular refurbishment on a scale befitting a grand establishment and deploying her own considerable design skills in supervising the changes.
This – to OG's mind – rather unnecessary intrusion may have led to occasional and spectacular rows, but undoubtedly did much to maintain for some time the Goring's reputation for comfort. Above all, she nursed her husband devotedly,

remaining to the end the embodiment of an ever-present help in trouble.

In contrast Penny, George's wife, has remained resolutely in the background. Her arrival in the family was at first fiercely resisted by her future parents-in-law, but in 1995, after thirty-three years of marriage, she had changed very little from the farmer's daughter who had captivated her husband-to-be in a stableyard in Cornwall. Her passion for horses is such that she was able to enthuse George to an extent that he too became a fanatic. Her dislike of urban life is deep-rooted: early married life in Chester Square while her husband was working his way through the managerial ranks of the Goring was purgatory, made bearable only by the thought of an early move to the country. Once that came about her rare appearances at the hotel were followed always by a prompt return to her Kent home. Staff at the Goring who have known her longest, however, describe her with patent sincerity 'as the best thing that ever happened to Mr George', and look forward to her visits with a touching eagerness. She and their country house have become the tranquil haven to which her husband is always able to return from his seemingly endless professional and social engagements, as well as from his forays into the more dangerous and eccentric reaches of equestrian activity. The fact that he makes that journey from London to Kent up to six evenings a week is eloquent testimony to their harmonious relationship. It is no coincidence that this happy family atmosphere affects almost tangibly the staff and guests of the Goring Hotel.

The Manager's Tale

The house telephone rang at the Goring front desk.

'Reception.'

'Suite 74.' The man's voice was strained. Almost tangible emotion flowed down the line. 'Get me the Manager, please.'

It was a Saturday afternoon and the young assistant manager on duty picked up his phone.

'Hullo, sir, Robert Gibbs here. Can I help?'

'Will you come up. Now.' It was an order.

'Certainly, sir. Is something wrong?'

'Better come and see.' The line clicked as he rang off.

Gibbs hurried to the lift. What was it, he wondered; why were the guests not at Wimbledon? That was why they had come to London for the weekend; indeed they had been to watch the tennis yesterday. The married couple in the suite were well known to the Goring. A successful businessman in the City and an attractive young wife; plenty of money; regular visitors. Was one of them ill? As he reached the door marked 74, he mentally reviewed the medical procedures. He knocked. No reply. Again. Not a sound. He felt for his pass-key and went inside.

The man was crouched in a corner, arms across his face as if warding off an attack. The room was a mess: furniture overturned, the television on its side on the floor. The manager paused as he took in the shambles. He saw blood on the walls. And hair. Blonde. The wife was blonde. He took another step and saw the body. She was curled up, and what he could see of her face through a terrifying mask of more blood and slowly matting hair, was blue, almost black. The man in the corner spoke.

'I've killed her,' he said. He began to sob.

Robert Gibbs retrieved the telephone from the bed. Ambulance and police arrived in urgent succession. They attended to the wife first. Not dead, they said. But close. She might – possibly – recover. They carried her away and the police took brief statements. Then they left with the man. 'I've killed her,' he said again.

But the ambulancemen were right. Their medical skills – and Gibbs's prompt action – had saved her life. The husband was charged with attempted murder, but in court the victim was adamant: an accident; a silly row; as much my fault as his. He didn't try to kill me. A two-year suspended sentence.

The wife's recovery was somewhat speedier than that of Suite 74; a complete redecoration was necessary. Carpet, curtains, chair covers and wallpaper – all had to be replaced. The cost was substantial and the Goring, after a decent interval, presented the account to the guest. He paid without demur, and came eventually to stay at the hotel again. But not in Suite 74 – and not with his wife.

Although no one has actually ever been murdered at the Goring, there have been two successful suicides. In the late 1950s a first-time guest booked in for just one night. There was nothing remarkable in his demeanour. He dined alone in the restaurant, reading a book and responding quietly and courteously to the waiters. He drank steadily, but not immoderately, a bottle of one of the more noble clarets and a glass or two of armagnac. Saying good night to the duty porters, he went to his room. The next morning the chambermaid let herself in. As he had told her he would be down to breakfast at nine she had expected no answer to her perfunctory knock. She found him in his bath; wrists slashed, the water red. Stifling a scream, she ran for Mrs Schoeffter.

Thirty years later Mary Davin, on her afternoon tour of inspection, heard moaning sounds coming from a single room. Looking at her records, she noted that a young woman had checked in the previous afternoon. She summoned the duty manager and they prepared to enter, but the door had been securely locked from the inside in a way which made the pass-key unworkable. There was now no sound from the room, and no response, either, to their repeated enquiries. The police were called, broke the door down and found the girl dead in her bed. The distressing signs of a planned suicide were plain to see, empty bottles of aspirin and brandy completing the picture. The young woman, whose husband had left her twenty-four hours earlier, had come to the Goring to die.

Death poses a very particular problem for the management team of any hotel. Discretion is paramount – little is as disturbing to a guest's general well-being as being confronted by a platoon of undertakers going about their business. The Goring method is to use the luggage lift at as quiet a time of day or night as the proprieties allow. Happily it is not a problem which has to be faced with any frequency; there have been only three deaths on the premises since 1960.

In life, as in death, the management style of the house of Goring has always been intensely personal. The size of the hotel, and the fact that all three proprietors in turn have been almost omnipresent, have precluded the rise of a General Manager of the stature of Branchini of Claridge's or the brothers Gelardi who ruled at the Ritz and the Savoy. Bassanetti, OR Goring's first General Manager, was little more than the most senior member of staff – there to take charge when the founder was away. And what with the need to establish his new hotel as being among the foremost in London, the inconvenient intrusion of the First World War, and his extension plans in the early twenties, OR was away very, very little.

The arrival of his son in 1924 as Bassannetti's successor and OG's subsequent elevation to Managing Director (same job, different title, but bringing occupation of one of the two seats on the Board), freed the older Goring from day-to-day administrative duties and, as the years rolled by, OG became the decision-maker in all but the most major aspects of company policy. He took his duties seriously. Exposure to the hotel scene across the Atlantic, and his subsequent employment as European correspondent for the *National Hotel Review of America*, brought him into contact with the novels and other writings of Sinclair Lewis, a winner of the Pulitzer Prize and, in 1930, the first American to be awarded the Nobel Prize for Literature. One of Lewis's many strengths was his ability to portray small-town America, and OG was so taken by the novelist's description, in an article, of what it takes to be a successful hotelier that he adopted it as his creed. This extract from the original has been paraphrased a little:

> You will have to learn manners, learn to be poker-faced with people who would take advantage of you. You will have to know all about china and silver, glass, linen, brocades and the best of woods for flooring and furniture. A hotel manager has to be a combination of *hausfrau*, chef, nurse, doctor, lawyer, upholsterer and walking directory who knows just where the Baptist Church is, what time the marriage-licence office opens and when the next train leaves for Hicksville.
>
> He has to be an accountant, linguist, quick-action laundryman, plumber, carpenter, heating engineer, speech-maker, cop that can tell from looking at a girl's ears whether she's married to the guy or not and money-lender – only he doesn't get any interest or have any security.
>
> He has to be better dressed than a Savile Row dummy and tell from a cow's moo whether she will make good steaks. He has to know more about wine and cigars than the guy who makes them and, all the time, he has to be a diplomat that would make the Secretary-General of the United Nations look like a football fan on a spree. He has to set a table like the Queen of England yet watch the pennies like an Arab pedlar. If you can do all this, you'll have a good time. Go to it.

OG went to it with a will, making these precepts his own and never losing an opportunity to impress them on the series of assistant managers that came and went over his fifty years at the Goring. Easily the most receptive was the twenty-five-year-old Norman Pennington, who arrived in 1938 and was to become what OG described as 'my right-hand man'. To many thousands of guests he was the very personification of the gentle good manners and self-effacing loyalty on which the Goring prided itself.

Norman Pennington had been a junior manager for barely a year when, with the coming of war, the call came for military duty. Rising in six years from private soldier to acting colonel, his military record was a measure of the man. By 1946 he was back at the Goring, and OG, mindful of the indelible impression he had made in a few short months and impressed by the senior rank he had attained, appointed him General Manager, at the same time initiating a system of engaging trainee managers for a year before encouraging them to move on to more responsible employment elsewhere. The British hotel industry has much to be grateful for in OG's assiduous concern that qualifications in the profession should be gained and recognized in the same way as those in, say, accountancy or engineering. Within the Goring itself, he accepted only the highest standards, and outside it he was tireless in promoting programmes of formal education in every aspect of the trade. He also foresaw the need to nurture home-grown talent to succeed the Continentals who had once held a virtual monopoly of senior hotel management in Britain. The Germans who had been prominent before the First World War had been replaced by Italians, but when, following the outbreak of war in 1939, they too were repatriated or interned as 'enemy aliens' (in 1940 hundreds were lost when the *Arandora Star*, a liner chartered to take the internees to Canada, was sunk), there was a gap which had to be filled. The difficulties were formidable. In 1941 there was only one hotel school in the country, the Westminster Technical Institute for Hotel Education, of which, needless to say, OG was a governor. As Chairman of the Hotel and Catering Institute after the war, he led the movement to persuade technical colleges to open faculties in hotel catering and management, and began to establish the system of examinations and subsequent membership gradings which gave the industry, for the first time, an official structure.

OG Goring and Norman Pennington together managed the Goring for twenty-four years, if not in perfect harmony, at least with a profound and ever-mindful understanding of their respective positions – particularly on Pennington's part. Mostly they complemented each other; Pennington's supreme administrative efficiency and palpable niceness endeared him to the staff, while his deferential air and old-world courtesy appealed alike to the county set and to the growing number of American guests. As has been said, however, OG's high regard – even respect – for his right-hand man did not extend to any notion of either social or professional equality. After a one-sided exchange of views in the presence of OG's personal assistant, Edwina Davy, during which the latter had been appalled by her employer's hectoring tone, she went to commiserate with Pennington. 'I suppose you think I'm something of a mouse, Davy,' he said quietly. 'But you have to remember that I have a wife and two daughters and live in a [Goring] house in Victoria Square. It would be very difficult for me if I found us all sitting on the pavement.'

Some of the more stressful moments of a manager's life stem from the enforcement of house rules and dealing politely but firmly with guests who attempt to flaunt them. The Goring has never had any truck with prostitutes – however discreet their disguise – and still, as the end of the century approaches, tries to ensure that a single room remains exactly that. Indeed, the entertainment of any non-residents in bedrooms is still actively discouraged, although night managers now have a wider discretion in deciding who is and is not a desirable visitor. There is another regulation, too, which guests occasionally find irksome. Pet animals are banned. A notice dated March 1910 is displayed in Reception. 'Visitors are respectfully reminded,' it reads, 'that dogs, cats, birds and other pets are not allowed in any part of this hotel.' The first recorded circumvention of this rule took place in 1912 when a lady wearing a large muff booked into a room with a balcony on the first floor. It was a warm night and she went to sleep leaving her windows open. By breakfast-time the next morning, the office was being bombarded with perplexed telephone calls. One guest reported that the bits and pieces on her dressing-table had been disarranged; another that his papers had been scattered to all corners of his room while a third, an elderly matron, rang to report the disappearance of her wig. After several more calls in similar vein, a man came down in the lift to say that he would never stay at the Goring again. He had awoken to find a marmoset sitting on the end of his bed; had the hotel perhaps turned into a zoo overnight? Both monkey and wig were eventually retrieved and the lady left – with an empty muff and her pet sitting on her shoulder.

In 1930 a regular guest arrived on his way home from a week's shooting in Scotland. He was known to have an uncertain temper, and when he introduced a red setter into the

hall, there was clearly going to be a problem. The Head Porter of the day, William Bingham, was given short shrift: 'Don't talk such bloody nonsense, man. Of course the dog's staying with me. Who the devil do you think you are? Fetch Goring.' OG was summoned, and got a full measure of the same: 'This is my dog, Goring. I've been coming here for years. Tell your man to take him to my room.'

Not without difficulty, OG was able to calm him down.

'I wonder, my lord,' he ventured after some time. 'I wonder, my lord, where you keep the dog at home?'

'In the kennels, of course. In the bloody ken – Ah. I see what you mean. Oh very well then, you look after him. Feed him, mind.' And OG led the animal off to the mews garage he kept for just such emergencies.

Things did not go quite so well when an American family, after staying for a fortnight, bought a valuable Yorkshire terrier to take home to the States in order to breed from it. The animal had been housed at Harrods for two days, but on their last day the family, due to leave on the early-morning boat-train, asked OG to deal with the dog's overnight keep. The terrier was led off to the makeshift quarters across the road to be fed, watered and bedded down by a cooing porter. When OG went to check on it first thing in the morning, the dog had gone leaving a long length of sash-cord attached to the wall. It had been bitten through. With only an hour to go before the departure of the owners, OG dared not ask them for a full description. He rang the police and did his best. It was mention of the sash-cord that rang reputation-saving bells. The dog had been captured in the gardens of Buckingham Palace and was now in custody. Someone would bring him round. OG's apprehensive vision of angry guests and – worse, much worse – the prospect of paying compensation and shipping a replacement across the Atlantic, receded. He was able to hand the dog over to its smiling owners only half an hour later.

Dealing with the attempted smuggling of pets – or even demurely disguised ladies of the night – into the Goring bedrooms is, however, small beer indeed on the scale of management skills when compared to accusations of theft. The first difficulty is sorting out the genuine from the imagined; the vast majority of alleged robberies of guests turn out to be

no more than the result of absent-mindedness. A man complains that his wallet has been stolen: 'I know it was with me in my room; the floor-waiter who brought me my breakfast must have taken it.' A cursory examination of his bedroom reveals that the guest had used the wallet to prop up his bedside light to a more convenient angle. Two women claim that one of them has been robbed of a roll of $500 bills: 'I can't possibly have lost it; I keep it tucked into my suspender at the top of my stocking.' That same day, the police ring to say a cab driver has handed in the wad, saying that he had picked up two ladies from the Goring Hotel. Did Mr Pennington know anything about it?

While robberies have happened, and doubtless will again, they are surprisingly few and far between. A relatively small hotel is able to keep a close, if largely unnoticed, watch on both its staff and its guests. A strange face in the wrong place at an inappropriate time stands out, and is likely to be commented upon. Inside jobs are very rare; pass-keys are carefully controlled and suspicion is quickly focused, usually correctly, on newcomers to the staff. From the outside even the most enterprising of burglars finds that gaining unobserved entry is difficult – although an impecunious German student did spend a night on Mary Scoggins's balcony overlooking Victoria Square when searching for somewhere safe to sleep. The rustling of his newspaper sheets awoke her at dawn. He was so clearly innocent of any criminal intent that she found it difficult to convince her friends that he was an entirely unauthorized guest!

More serious than the plain forgetfulness of guests was an incident concerning Les Nicol, at the time an employee of over thirty years' standing. He had left the concierge's desk one evening to have supper, handing over to one of the floor-waiters. A woman, arriving for dinner, asked if she could leave her mink stole in the latter's charge and the floor-waiter, not wanting to hang it in the public cloakroom, put it in Nicol's cupboard. He forgot to tell the concierge, however, and in due course went off duty. Shortly afterwards, Tipper locked his cupboard and handed over his desk to the night staff, he too then went home. At 3 am he was woken by the police. They refused to tell him what it was they wanted, asking him only whether he 'was in charge of the cloakroom of the Goring Hotel' and demanding to search his house. Finding nothing, they asked for his hotel keys. Nicol refused to hand them over and went with them to the Goring. Their attitude was upsettingly hostile – not at all what he was used to from the usually friendly and co-operative force stationed at Rochester Row. He opened his cupboard and saw the stole for the first time. Refusing to hand it over until he had a receipt, he went to the station to make a statement and then demanded that the police take him home. The next morning the floor-waiter, stricken with contrition, confirmed the sequence of events and the Goring management, led by a vengeful OG, demanded an apology of the police. This was rapidly – and handsomely – forthcoming from the very top, for the owner of the mink was a close friend of the Chief Commissioner of the Metropolitan Police, and had not hesitated to pull strings.

The arrival of George Goring in 1962 threw an uncertain spanner into the well-oiled management machinery. Norman Pennington had been dreading this moment. He had known for years that one day the young heir would have to come and be schooled in the Goring ways, eventually to supersede him but he had not been told exactly how this would affect his own future. Would he be downgraded from the general managership? Would he, perhaps, even be asked to leave? His position, never in his own mind entirely secure, now seemed terminally in peril – the loss of his job a matter only of time. He had, it was true, been made an associate director but this had only resulted in his name being added to the heading of the official Goring writing-paper. He did not sit on the Board; the only directors with real power were OG and Edna. And, on a lower level, although just as important to this unhappy man, was the question of how his daily routine might be affected? He was a man of habit, cherishing the timetable he set for himself, and sticking to it religiously. Every morning he arrived from No. 2 Victoria Square bang on the dot of 9; an hour for lunch with Nellie his wife, back at precisely 2 pm, and home again at 6. Each day he consulted with Chef at 9.15 and checked the cellar at 10. On Fridays at 11, he went to the bank to collect the cash and make up the wages. Everything was done by the book – his book. Change would be unwelcome; innovation threatening.

In the event, he discovered that he had nothing to worry about. OG would have never dreamt of getting rid of him, and Mr George, whose official title was Assistant Manager, was the model of hard-working, deferential tact. In fact, George's arrival in many ways bolstered Pennington's confidence. In young Mr Goring he found an ally, especially in giving voice to measures for improving the lot of the staff, and thus the efficiency of the hotel, which he himself would never have dared to suggest to OG. For example, there was the matter of regular meetings with Heads of Department: Chef, Housekeeper, Concierge, Head Waiter, and so on. It had occurred to Pennington more than once that it would be useful if they could all meet regularly with management as a body, thereby doing away with the need for separate interviews and time-consuming inter-departmental memos. Such an arrangement would also give the staff a chance to air small grievances which could then be nipped in the bud before they became contentious. George put this to OG who, predictably, would have none of it. 'If you get them all together, all they'll do is find ways of asking for more money. Out of the question.'

The new-found allies persisted, however, and it was eventually arranged that meetings would take place once a month. A handsomely bound minute book was bought ('More waste of money'). At the first of the gatherings no one was prepared to speak as OG sat silently glowering. After some time Pennington, prompted by George, brought up the matter of staff pensions, which were then being introduced into the industry elsewhere. OG skilfully swept the business under the carpet. At the conclusion he was furious and refused to sign the minutes. 'What did I tell you? More money – that's all they want. I shall never come to another of these performances.' But despite his opposition the system took root; regular staff meetings were soon to be held at every level. OG, though, stuck to his word; he never again allowed himself to be faced formally by his employees. In any case, he now had a very different but major preoccupation to engage him.

In 1964, Westminster Council decided to rename that part of Ebury Street in which the Goring stood. The stretch of road between the Royal Mews and Grosvenor Gardens was to be called Beeston Place and, worse, was to become a one-way street. In this measure OG discerned both an opportunity and a potential disaster. He tackled the name-change first. If the title of the street largely occupied by his hotel was to be changed, the obvious choice was Goring Place. And, furthermore, the council should remember that it was a Goring who had built a house on the site of Buckingham Palace long before the eponymous Duke got his hands on the land. He put this to the council but his case was rejected – Beeston being a village in Cheshire particularly dear to the hearts (and no doubt the head) of the Grosvenor family, whose roots are in that county. He put it to them again; again they said no. He camped in the council offices – if his father, by sheer persistence, could persuade the old Duke of Westminster to change his mind and sell the original site of the hotel, then surely he could bend a lot of mere local politicians to his will? But the opposition was implacable.

He next turned his attention to the one-way street problem. Such a diversion of traffic would restrict access to the Goring; his guests would find it inconvenient; taxis would not be so readily available to his doormen. Again he failed to get the decision rescinded, but his death in 1974 at least spared him the worst repercussions when the deregulation of bus routes made Beeston Place an irresistible attraction for traffic from Victoria Coach Station – the largest such terminus in Europe – as a route north and west out of the capital. Horrendous traffic jams ensued, and George Goring was to fight for over ten years until, finally, both coaches and lorries were banned from the street, making it again one of the quietest in Central London. OG would have been proud of his son's tenacity.

Norman Pennington died in 1970, the victim of a pernicious cancer which allowed him only six weeks from diagnosis to death. He had, fortuitously, made provision for his wife Nellie and his daughters, having bought a house in the suburbs some years earlier. His gentle ways and straightforward character, as well as his bravery in continuing to try to struggle on with his duties from his sickbed, had made him a much-loved figure, respected by both guests and staff. They and the whole Goring family recognized that an important era had died with him. But it was now time to look to the future.

A key figure in that future had already arrived late in 1969 in the shape of the tall, elegant William Cowpe. A Lancashireman, he was in part a product of the educational system for the profession which OG had so assiduously promoted. After studying hotel management he had gone on to work in some of the great hotels of Europe: the Savoy in London, the Château d'Ouchy in Lausanne, and the Kur Hotel in Bad Neuenahr. While in Germany, someone had recommended the Goring to him,and he wrote for an interview. He was asked to telephone for an appointment when he arrived in England, and when he did call from Heathrow, George Goring, characteristically, told him to come straight round. The two young men got on well – it was more of a chat than an interview as they compared experiences on the Continent – and George finally asked him to start in a month. It was only some time later that Cowpe discovered that the

Goring had not been in need of an assistant manager – a vacancy had been created especially for him.

By this time OG was in a wheelchair, condemned to spending his days being nursed at home at Court Lodge. George and Norman Pennington were effectively running the Goring and William was put to work in each department in turn, gaining experience in all aspects of the hotel's administration. He had privately decided that the Goring would be an excellent place in which to gain a solid grounding, but that it was really rather old-fashioned – handwritten accounts, the absence of television or even radios from the bedrooms, and the creaking telephone system, all astonished him. There were few signs of the modern technology that he had been led to believe was essential. But he noticed too that the occupancy rates were quite extraordinarily high, and decided that this was probably the principle reason why OG and Norman Pennington seemed so adamantly resistant to change. He also observed that this unwillingness to spend money on improvements seemed to irk the owner's son.

Pennington's death was the catalyst for change. George announced that he was to become the General Manager; William Cowpe would be his deputy and another junior would be recruited. This rearrangement of responsibilities gave Cowpe pause for thought. He would now have greater responsibility; he discerned in George a desire for modernization that equalled his own, and he was not unmindful of the fact that it was reasonable to suppose that in the not too distant future OG, because of his health, would have to give up the reins of proprietorship altogether. William liked the Goring, admired the staff, and saw now why its rooms were always full. Suddenly there seemed little reason to move on. He felt confident that he and George would make a good team. He decided to stay.

7 *The Guest's Tale*

OG Goring Esq
The Goring Hotel
Ebury Street, London SW1

My dear Goring, *10 February 1960*
How very good of you to invite my wife and myself to your Golden Jubilee celebrations in March. As you know I am now confined to my bed here in Devon and sadly we shall not be able to attend.

I have very fond memories of that day fifty years ago when your father welcomed us at the door and explained that we were to be his first patrons. How things have changed since then! Two world wars, millions of motor-cars and aeroplanes everywhere – even in our skies down here.

Mrs Moore and I have always enjoyed our stays at the Goring and have watched your progress with interest. At least with you some things have never changed. It is always comforting to be met by the same old faces and I hope Nicol is keeping well. It is hard to believe that it is thirty years since he was a page-boy. I expect he will be with you for some time yet.

Please give our very best wishes to all our old friends and we send kindest regards to your wife and Mr Pennington.

With best wishes, I am yours etc,
LR Moore, Colonel (Retd)

In November 1910 four young men, newly down from Oxford, were travelling by train to London for a Law Society dinner. They were discussing the problem of where to stay that night. One of them, Alexander Watson, mentioned that a smashing new hotel had opened in Belgravia, and that it had a bathroom with every bedroom. 'Why don't we go there?' he suggested. The others demurred; Stuart Truell and John Lauder (son of the Scottish singer, Sir Harry) thought that it might be too expensive. Even Ashley Player – of the cigarette-manufacturing family – was uncertain: 'The thing is, Watson old boy, I haven't much money with me. Would they accept a bank draft, d'ye think?'

In the event the four friends took a single room each at a cost of 7s 6d (37½p., nominally; today, about £20 in real terms). All became regular visitors, and Alexander Watson was still staying periodically at the Goring fifty years later.

Dear Mr Goring, *June 1995*
My grandfather, Peter G Thompson spent his honeymoon with my step-grandmother (his second wife) at the Goring in 1923. My father, Alexander Thompson, my mother and four children, of whom I was the youngest, arrived together with an older cousin in August 1928 after a North Cape cruise and had the entire top floor with sitting rooms and four bedrooms. Bingham, the Hall Porter, arranged many sightseeing trips and even fixed a 'red-coat' [i.e. a Pensioner] from the Royal Hospital in Chelsea to show us around. When not out I used to play dinkie toys with a page called Fred [Scott] who was still there at my last visit in the early 1960s.

One night on my mother's birthday at the end of the month, we all went to dine at Scott's Restaurant, still on Piccadilly Circus then and I got tiddly sampling the grown-ups' wine. Father took me home to the Goring where Miss Wilkins the Housekeeper put me to bed and stayed with me until the gang got back.

We all had breakfast in our rooms and I had never encountered rolls, butter curls in a silver dish, English bacon and the best jams and marmalades before. Lunch in the dining-room was even more thrilling: waiters in tails and black ties, a round table with starched linen and fresh flowers. I always ate the same dessert – a biscuit tortini – and the only things I didn't like were the gravies (thinner) and the mashed potato (firmer) than I was used to.

In 1956 my wife and I came over on a package and were allotted a different hotel - not bad but not like the Goring. We used to come over to you for tea every day. In 1960, with our boys then 17 and 14 and our daughter aged 10 together with two friends of our sons, we came to the Goring and took over a whole row on the front of the building. Very little had changed but the street was a little noisier. The indispensable Fred took care of our excess belongings when we toured Britain and pulled a real coup when he got my wife (who doesn't fly – ever) a first-class seat on a train to Glasgow on a Bank Holiday Saturday night.

A little later, my wife and I bought a small cottage in Sussex and lived there off and on for six years. I cannot remember the number of times we came back to you for meals, to meet friends and stay the odd night. There is this the corner of our memories that is for ever England – the Goring Hotel.

Most sincerely,
Chilton Thompson
Cleveland, Ohio, USA

One of the few regrets in the life of Otto Gustave Goring was that his father had not bought a visitors' book. Had he done so, the early days of the hotel would have recorded some priceless memories. In June 1911, it would have registered the presence of some twenty royal personages and their suites during the Coronation of King George V – the first occasion on which the Goring was annexed by Buckingham Palace as an overflow for its guests. In 1912 the signatures of Kaiser Wilhelm II and his German courtiers would have appeared, for they stayed at the hotel during the then German Emperor's unsuccessful mission to change the King's mind over the latter's personal assurance to Prince Henry of Prussia (the

Kaiser's brother) that, in the event of Austria and Germany going to war with Russia and France, Britain would come to the assistance of her allies

It was not until 1934 that OR was persuaded and a fine leather-bound, gold-tooled volume was acquired – just in time for the marriage of the Duke of Kent to Princess Marina of Greece. The very first entries show the signatures of royal guests from Greece, Yugoslavia and Denmark, as well as that of James Craig – later, as Viscount Craigavon, the first Prime Minister of Northern Ireland – and the single word 'Cambrensis', signifying the Archbishop of Wales. The Archbishop, Dr Charles Green, was a regular at the Goring; indeed OG had entertained hopes that he would officiate at his wedding to Edna, an ambition thwarted when Mrs Green died suddenly just before the event.

The Goring's visitors' book has been sparingly deployed, a mere five pages being used up from its inception to the outbreak of the Second World War. Qualification for entry is stringent. Royalty of course, politicians (but only those regarded by the Goring as statesmen), ambassadors, some very senior officers of the armed services, and a few carefully selected celebrities, ranging from Sir Adrian Boult to Wimbledon champion Bill Tilden, grace the early entries. Lord Mottistone who, as Sir John Seely had been Secretary of State for War during the Curragh Mutiny of the army in Ireland in 1914, was a frequent visitor, having first stayed at the Goring during the Great War while on leave from the trenches of the Western Front, to which he had repaired to command a Canadian cavalry brigade after his resignation from the Government. 'I will never forget it,' he used to tell an avid OG. 'I got in from France in such a disgusting state that one of your valets put me in a bath fully clothed to soften me up, and then proceeded to delouse me.'

Sir Austen and Lady Chamberlain (the half-brother of Neville, the Conservative Prime Minister, with whom he was not on speaking terms as the Second World War approached) lived at the Goring for two years, receiving a number of pro-rearmament politicians, including Winston Churchill and Anthony Eden. Churchill himself was already an old habitué of the hotel (in which his mother-in-law had a room) and lived there for several months in 1937, acquiring a reputation among the staff as a fractious and somewhat ill-tempered guest. He had, it may be supposed, even then a great deal else on his mind.

Other residents during the 1930s whose signatures appear include Sir Hughe and Lady Knatchbull-Hugessen. Sir Hughe was convalescing at the Goring having been shot at and wounded during an attack by a Japanese aeroplane while serving as British Ambassador to China (which Japan had invaded) from 1936 to 1938. Two years later he went on to Turkey, again as Ambassador, where his otherwise distinguished service was marred by the activities of the spy Richard Sorge, an Albanian known by the code-name 'Cicero', who, ostensibly employed as the valet at the British Embassy, was busily passing his master's secrets to the German High Command.

Not all diplomats are asked to sign the book. One who did not qualify (not yet senior enough) was a Frenchman who had arranged to marry into the English peerage. The lady would be his second wife, and since she too had been married before, he asked the Goring to book in both sets of immediate family for the fortnight preceding the wedding. 'I have,' he explained to an incredulous Norman Pennington, 'I have eight children, all over twenty years old, and my fiancée has six. Her youngest is seventeen. I wish to take a whole floor. What can you do?' What Pennington was able to do, once he had recovered his composure, was to range the diplomat's family on one side of the corridor and place the lady and her children in rooms immediately opposite. Diplomacy indeed.

Bottled sauces are rarely demanded in the dining room of the Goring Hotel, and are certainly never in evidence. An exception was made in the case of Mr Perrins, whose ancestors, together with their friends and partners, the Leas, had invented the famous Worcestershire Sauce, and who would occasionally enquire, diffidently, whether his concoction was on hand. The Head Waiter of the day, Toni Perilli, learnt to keep a bottle in his cupboard and, on the receipt of the code-word 'Worcester' flashed to him by an alert concierge, would produce it with a flourish as its manufacturer entered the dining-room. Not so easy to please, however, was the formidable Lady Palmer, scion of one half of the twinned families of biscuit makers, Huntley and Palmer. OG Goring was fussy about his cheese biscuits, insisting on serving his guests with what he considered to be the best, and to his mind the best was undoubtedly the product of the rival company, Carr's. Furthermore, Carr's packed their biscuits in handily sized quarter tins, a quantity which helped keep them fresh and led to minimum waste. This arrangement particularly appealed to the careful OG and it was not until Huntley and Palmer agreed to follow suit – presumably at the behest of Lady Palmer – that he bought some of her own product as an alternative. Thereafter her entrance into the hotel was also signalled to the dining room, so that all overt traces of Carr's could be conjured from sight.

Sir Reginald Wingate, Governor-General of the Sudan for seventeen years and British High Commissioner in Egypt from 1917 to 1919 was eighty when he came to live at the Goring during the Second World War. He became a great favourite of the staff, and in 1947 went to stay with OG and Edna at their house in Kent. There, on St George's Day, the old boy took the salute at a march-past of the local Boy Scout troop, a far cry from the thousands of troops he had been accustomed to reviewing in the Sudan, and yet an occasion which led him to murmur to his host, 'We could have done with a few of these at the Battle of Omdurman.'

Wingate's nephew Orde, the gifted, extraordinarily brave but eccentric general, who until his death in an aircraft accident, led the Chindit infiltration operations behind Japanese lines in Burma during 1943-44, flew to England to be interviewed by Churchill and make a report to King George VI. He stepped off his aircraft and drove straight to the Goring to have lunch with his uncle. OG was scandalized. 'He was dirty,' he reported later to Edna. 'He hadn't shaved or bathed or changed – still wearing his shorts and boots and a jungle hat. And he didn't even wash before he went to the Palace. Unworthy of an officer, in my opinion.'

Dear Sir, *June 1995*

My husband and I met when we were both living in London in 1936. We were married later that year at Christ Church, Westminster (bombed during the war and now a grassy bank) and had our reception at the Goring where my family were staying.

We celebrated both our silver and golden anniversaries at the hotel and if my husband had not sadly died three months ago we would undoubtedly have had our diamond wedding party there. The Goring family has created an oasis in London and friends from Canada and Australia always stay there when they come over – it is a very special place.

Yours faithfully,
Stella Brecknell
Dolphin Square, London

The Children's Encyclopaedia, The Children's Newspaper, A Thousand Heroes, and a number of other scientific and natural-history works for children were all created by Arthur Henry Mee in Room 38 of the Goring, in which he lived from 1920 until shortly before his death in 1943. OG was fascinated by this one-man accumulation of knowledge and came to know Mee well, spending hours in his room watching the author at work. In 1922 they listened together to one of the first crystal (cat's-whisker) wireless sets picking up transmissions from the embryonic British Broadcasting Company and OG was astonished to discover that at midnight, when the station closed down as Big Ben marked the hour, he was able to hear all twelve strokes on Mee's apparatus before the sound of the final toll reached Room 38 in real time (a circumstance explained by the relatively slow speed of sound compared to the speed at which radio waves travel). Residents of the Goring in rooms facing south-east can still experience this phenomenon on more modern receivers. Even the roar of London's traffic fails to quench the chimes of Big Ben at midnight.

It was once the practice of London's evening newspapers to publish lists of 'Americans Staying at London Hotels'. Those staying at the Berkeley, Claridge's, the Savoy, the Ritz, the Mayfair, the Dorchester and the Goring filled many column inches daily supplemented from time to time by 'Visitors from the Dominions'. It was not, apparently, deemed necessary to detail those from Europe, and nor was there a regular account of British guests, other than those whose importance warranted a mention in the Court Circulars of *The Times* and the *Daily Telegraph and Morning Post*. Thus, in January 1935, it was reported that: 'Prince and Princess Viggo, Count and Countess Rosenborg are staying at the Goring Hotel, Belgravia. They visited Their Majesties and remained to Luncheon.' And the same year: 'The Prime Minister of Northern Ireland and Viscountess Craigavon expect to arrive at the Goring Hotel, Grosvenor Gardens, SW1 (telephone Victoria 8210) on Saturday the 1st of May from Stormont Castle, Belfast.'

Also in 1935, although unremarked by the newspapers, Miss Rosie Myers came to stay. Unlike her distinguished fellow guests, Miss Myers was to maintain her residence for nearly

thirty years. Short and plump, she lived in Room 33, entirely oblivious to bombs, blackouts and food shortages during the war, going out for her daily walks and evening theatre trips wearing, always, one of a selection of enormously wide-brimmed hats in which she resembled, quite unmistakably, a perambulating mushroom. As she grew older so her girth expanded, until the day came when she stuck in her bath. Miss Myers lay like a half-beached whale until at last she heard her breakfast arriving and was able to summon help by shouting through the locked door. Norman Pennington, loath to break the door down for fear of alarming the old lady, sent a valet on a precarious journey along a narrow outside balustrade until he was able to gain access through the bathroom window. Extricating Miss Myers, however, proved beyond his strength – every time he thought he had her, she would slip, gasping, through his hands, her little black eyes tightly shut, as if believing that if she could not see him, then he would be unable to see her resplendently naked body. Eventually, three of the housekeeping staff managed to heave her out and Pennington, secretly, had special locks fitted to her bathroom door to ensure easy entry during further emergencies – of which, in the event, there were many.

It was Miss Myers's custom to take breakfast in her room, descending afterwards to the ground floor where she would always head for the ladies' lavatory, a ritual which, in her later years, became something of a trial for the hall porters. For she

would invariably emerge with her voluminous skirts tucked in to her knickers at the back, so that it became a matter of honour among the staff to creep up on her and release them without their owner being aware that her person was being tampered with. As she grew older still, she developed two all-consuming fears, first that her diamond watch would stop – an unthinkable eventuality which she warded off by handing it to Tipper Nicol for winding every morning – and, desperately, that she would one day become bedridden and have to leave the hotel. OG repeatedly assured her that she could stay as long as she wished and that, if necessary, special arrangements would be made. When finally she fell so ill that her doctor ordered her to hospital, she asked her stretcher-bearers to pause in the hall so that she could address the assembled staff: 'I don't want to be a nuisance, Mr Goring,' she said. 'You have all been so good to me. I don't think I shall be coming back.' She died that night.

Rosie Myers might have been a trifle eccentric, but she had nothing on another long-term resident, Mrs Violet d'Arcy. Mrs d'Arcy's first name appeared to be a catalyst for her most obvious obsession for she dressed entirely in violet, and even provided her own violet sheets and pillow-cases. She also wrote in violet ink on violet paper – thereby rendering her messages invisible and causing the staff to open all her outgoing mail to place her letters in envelopes which could at least be read at the post office. On one day, never to be forgotten, she electrified a full lunchtime dining room by entering and standing stock-still until her startling appearance slowly silenced the guests. One by one they looked up to take in the vision confronting them. Assured of the full attention of her captive audience, Mrs d'Arcy spoke: 'This place,' she announced, 'is full of either witches or bitches. I shall lunch in my room.'

Trygve Lie, the Norwegian lawyer, politician and Secretary-General of the United Nations – the first to hold that post – from 1946 to 1952, made his London home at the Goring; indeed, he received notice of his appointment to head the UN while staying at the hotel. He became a personal friend of OG and always arrived accompanied by a suitcase full of delicacies quite unobtainable in postwar England. During his frequent

visits, caviare, foie gras and truffles became brief but unadvertised additions to the Goring menu, delighting not only Monsieur Gasc but also all those lucky enough to be let into the secret by a beaming OG.

As rationing eased, Gasc's talents flourished, with the result that a newly appointed British Ambassador to the USSR was so impressed by the excellence of the little Frenchman's dishes that he commissioned OG to supply the Moscow Embassy with regular food parcels, both to vary the monotony of the Russian diet and to impress his dinner guests with the quality of produce available in England. Boxes of hams, beef, lamb, potted shrimps, shellfish, cream and cheeses, carefully selected by OG from the best he could lay his hands on, were flown to Moscow to stock the Embassy's deep-freezes. The Goring's proprietor always felt that in this way the Goring was playing a vital role in improving Anglo-Soviet relations.

Dear Mr Goring, *June 1995*

Towards the end of the war I was in the Wrens [Women's Royal Naval Service] and had to meet my cousin, a Boy Seaman aged 17, from South Africa, to bring him home with me to Cambridge. His train was late at Victoria and we decided to stay the night and went to the Goring. The staff said that the hotel was full but, in fact I think they either suspected we were up to no good or that my cousin in sailor's uniform didn't quite fit in.

Anyway we were about to leave when a familiar face appeared at the Reception Desk. It was my brother-in-law, a Naval Officer, with a woman who was most definitely not my sister! We stared at each other as he handed in his keys and from that day to this we have never mentioned the matter to each other or anyone else!

Yours sincerely,
Katherine Round, Cambridge

The names of most of the vast number of famous people who have stayed at the Goring during its first eighty-seven years must, necessarily, remain unpublished. The majority choose the hotel not just for its standards of personal service, but also for the anonymity assured to them by its discreet staff.

Every Prime Minister (and a number of near misses) since Winston Churchill has been a guest, and the ends of at least three national coal, rail and Post Office strikes have been patiently negotiated in its private rooms. Statesmen from a variety of nations have met together to hammer out international agreements, senior members of the royal family, including the Queen and the Queen Mother, have been entertained to private parties, and an inexhaustible supply of celebrities have sought refuge from the inevitable publicity attendant on staying at one of the more media-conscious hotels.

Sir Michael Redgrave spent the final months of his life at the Goring, surrounded by his family during his last Christmas as he gradually slipped away, a victim of Alzheimer's disease. Other theatrical figures have maintained a higher public profile, notably the Crazy Gang, for years a resident act at the Victoria Palace, who used the Goring as their headquarters, as did Lupino Lane, composer of 'The Lambeth Walk' and star of *Me and My Girl* during the Second World War. Principal players from the Victoria Palace have often lived at the Goring (Arthur Lowe, the seemingly indestructible Captain Mainwaring of the television series *Dad's Army*, invariably fell asleep in the dining room over his breakfast porridge), while other actors and actresses, including Elizabeth Taylor, whose glass the barman would allow no one else to use, would host post-performance parties there. Sir Anthony Hopkins had his wedding reception at the hotel, while, from an earlier age, the American baritone and film star of the 1930s Nelson Eddy, had to be asked to leave his room, not because his singing in the bath kept other guests awake, but because he so repeatedly flooded his bathroom floor that the ceiling began to suffer.

The Goring has also long been a favourite of the Anglican Church – the signatures of a number of Archbishops of Canterbury grace the pages of the visitors' book – so much so that successive delegations of American bishops to the Lambeth Conference, held once every ten years, have put up at the hotel. They became such popular visitors that OG twice took them all to Court Lodge for the weekend. Tipper Nicol, at his desk during one of these conferences, was approached by an Englishman who asked whether the Bishop of California was about. 'I think so, sir,' he said. 'That'll be Bishop Block, I expect; the trouble with bishops is that they all have two names. Who shall I say is asking for him?' The man smiled. 'Fisher,' he said. 'Or if you like, you can call me Cantuar.'

Even in the 1990s the Goring retains some of the look and the feel of a place where people come and stay in comfort. But the restaurant is so popular that when I telephoned to book two days before, I got the last free table.

We had our pre-lunch drinks in the uncluttered luxury of the

lounge. On the rug in front of the fire lay a couple of realistic sheep, a ewe and a lamb I gather, which reassuringly turned out to be stuffed. Always a good guide as to how a place sees itself, the pictures are subdued landscapes and seascapes, apparently originals, just the sort of thing a squire might hang on his walls. While you peer at them you can nibble cheese straws, which I thought a vanished dainty . . . *Kingsley Amis*
April 1993

Dear Mr Goring, *July 1995*
I was pleased to see in the International Herald Tribune *that a book is to be written about the Goring. As you know I used to visit you a lot when Vice-President of my company in the eighties and we had our London headquarters in Stag Place. From the beginning I realized the quality and consistency of your kitchen and used your fine restaurant as the 'Best of British' to entertain overseas and continental guests.*

For my private pleasure I and some special friends often celebrated the Fall at the Goring with a grouse lunch and a great Burgundy. Your grouse has always been the most excellent in England – year in, year out!

You ought to know that a lady with a very senior position in my company has also fond memories of the Goring – she was a maid with you for a while when she arrived in London to start her studies in accountancy. You had a hard-working genius right there in your midst and gave her the economics to start on her future career. Thank you.

Sincerely,
F Lee Faust
Berwyn, Pennsylvania, USA

Very little touches the hearts of the Goring staff more readily than an old-fashioned romance – and preferably one which culminates in a wedding reception held at the hotel. Such occasions are never forgotten:

Dear Goring family, *July 1995*
We were absolutely thrilled to receive such a really gorgeous bouquet of summer flowers on our Golden Wedding anniversary. How kind and thoughtful of you. They are still giving us

immense pleasure and remind us of our old garden in the country. Thank you so very much.

Yours sincerely,
Philomena Baynes
Sloane Court, London SW3

In more recent years the hotel has been riveted by a (so far) unrequited romance, and the fingers of staff are firmly crossed as they hope fervently for a happy ending. The principals are two Japanese academics working at one of England's oldest universities. He is a professor, she a doctor; both are in their late twenties. Every year for the past five years he has booked a suite for a week and, opposite it, a single room. From London's leading florist he fills the suite with roses, and there installs his lady love. He occupies the single room. Every year he proposes, but so far, to the disappointment of a staff agog with anticipation and a management standing by with appropriately special champagne, she has failed to succumb. The sense of anticlimax as he pays his account with a rueful smile and a patient shrug of his shoulders, is palpable. The staff heave a collective and sentimental sigh as they wish them well: 'Next year, next year,' they whisper to him as he makes his forlorn departure. 'She must say yes next year.'

This cliff-hanging saga runs and runs but some love affairs are more swiftly resolved. A film star staying with his wife in that very same suite, disappeared one night with a male floor-waiter. Neither has ever returned.

Whatever the joys of romance, however, everything at the hotel has to be paid for. In 1938 Mr and Mrs Wareham spent the first night of their honeymoon at the Goring, paying £1.7s.6d. for their room and 9s. for breakfast (£1.37½ and 45p. respectively). In 1946, Mr and Mrs Phelips paid a room-rate of £1.15s. (£1.75), while the price of breakfast had mysteriously come down to 8s. (40p.) – an increase overall of some 19 per cent in eight years or 2.4 per cent a year, about half the rate of inflation of the early 1990s, but still surprising for an era of supposed financial stability.

On 21 April 1931 Owen Marriner, now of Upminster, was given a small twenty-first birthday dance at the hotel. There were thirty-four guests (among them the actor Jack Hawkins) and the final bill was £48.13s.6d., a price which included the cost of four suppers for the orchestra. This represents, with a service charge, about £1.10s. (£1.50) a head, and although typical of London's leading places of the period, seems ludicrously small, being hardly more than that paid by the Warehams for a room seven years later. The gap between the cost of food and drink and the nightly room-rate has widened spectacularly in sixty years – in the 1990s a party such as Mr Marriner's in a private dining room could hardly be priced at less than £60 a head, while a double room and breakfast would approach £200.

Dear Sir, *August 1995*

I have been sent the announcement about the Goring Hotel book, a friend in England assuming that being a regular guest since thirty-five years, there would be some reminiscences. However, much as I squeeze my memory there is nothing, no special event worthy to be published. Maybe one incident.

I had to visit a client of mine in Gillingham, Dorset and asked the Hall Porter to procure for me a rail ticket. However, I received a ticket for Gillingham in Kent. When I refused to take it, the young man said: 'I am sorry, Sir I thought you had made a mistake. No one goes to Gillingham in Dorset!' How could I be angry with him?

From checking in to checking out after eight to ten days every year everything was always working so smoothly, so polite and personal, everything happened on a cheerful basis, the personnel always greeting you by name. Peter and Freddie and Ernest in the hall; they have a natural feeling of which story, which joke can be narrated to which guest. I believe that the missing of incidents is due to the fact that the Goring is, you may call it, a family hotel, not in the meaning of a hotel for your family (which it is of course!) but that guests and the long-serving staff are just one family.

Yours faithfully,
Dr Hanspeter Hostettler
Zurich, Switzerland

8 *Mr George's Tale*

Barbara was the first and, as is the way with sheep, her family soon began to grow. She had first taken George Goring's fancy in 1987, when he saw her in the workshop of a Somerset furniture maker. With her beautifully carved wooden head, and clad in snowy-white fleece, she came to the hotel to take her place in the lounge, curled up in front of the fire. Tucked in alongside her, nose to little black nose, is a lamb, and scattered about in the most privileged of the bedrooms are some thirty more of their kind. It is George's ambition – one no doubt enthusiastically shared by his supplier – that in the fullness of time, a flock of one hundred Barbaras will lie contentedly about, pleasing his guests and adding another dimension to his and the Goring's already marked air of individuality. The determination which will ensure that this relatively modest aspiration is fulfilled has been replicated throughout most of both his public and private life in the usually successful, and always dogged, pursuit of far grander and more difficult enterprises. It was not always so, however – as a boy, George Goring came perilously close to having the spirit irretrievably knocked out of him.

The twins, George and Richard, were born at the Goring barely a year before the outbreak of the Second World War. Schooldays were not in their case the happiest of their lives. After preparatory school in Kent, where they had to board from the age of seven because of petrol rationing, they went on to Cheltenham College,which they hated. Both boys were partially-sighted and wore pebble glasses – since replaced by contact lenses. Hardly able to see the blackboard and lying awake at night in adjoining beds nursing a terror of being caught out calling each other by their first names instead of by the regulation 'Goring G' and 'Goring R', they were slow learners. For this tardiness they were regularly beaten, and their misery was compounded by the fact that, because of their poor eyesight, they were unable to play a full part in the team games which, to others stuck firmly at the bottom of the academic ladder, offered a welcome alternative route to Establishment approval. Their parents, seeking to ease their sons' way by currying favour with a sadistic housemaster, gave the man a bullterrier puppy. The plan failed, however, as the animal was given to defecating daily on the dormitory floor and George and Richard were made to clean up the mess. Neither brother can recall ever receiving a word of praise, or even of encouragement, in their efforts to please; yet despite the constant abuse it is remarkable how little this extended period of abject misery appears to have affected the twins. On the contrary, George would claim, it had the positive benefit of instilling within him a determination always to try harder, to do better, never to give in. Certainly the will to succeed has characterized the lives of both twins.

Leaving Cheltenham after struggling to pass a set of fairly undistinguished O level examinations, the twins parted company. Richard, destined to take on his mother's family business, went to the Brixton School of Building, then acknowledged to be among the best in the world, while George, at his father's insistence, enrolled at the École Hôtelière in Lausanne. Until this moment, however, he had not given the hotel business much thought; indeed, the prospect of more school – even in Switzerland – appalled him. He had vaguely imagined that one day he might have to run the Goring, but how he was to go about preparing himself for that moment did not appear to be of immediate concern. What he wanted to do now was to get as far away from the horrors of school as he could possibly manage – travel perhaps; see the world.

His father had no such accommodating notions. George needed to learn the business, and where better than at Europe's leading establishment, where he himself had been so many years ago? They agreed a compromise: George would go to Lausanne for a year. He would do a foundation course and learn to speak French. He would also study restaurant management – training in both the kitchens and on the restaurant floor. Detailed hotel administration could wait – it was, OG considered, better taught in England by now anyway.

Despite his apprehensions, George enjoyed Lausanne. His French, the language in which all tuition and examination took place, became fluent, and by the end of his year he found that he could not bear the thought of returning to England. Instead he disappeared for six months, sending his parents a postcard to say that he would contact them soon. From Lausanne he went to Libya and then to Tunis, where he worked for a while in the Palace Hotel. When, in 1956, bombs began to fall on Alexandria as French and British troops invaded Egypt in an ill-judged and disastrous attempt to secure the Suez Canal, which Egypt, under its President, Nasser, had annexed, he caught a boat to Marseilles and found a job on a Swedish cargo ship plying its trade between Mediterranean ports and the east coast of the United States. He was officially engaged as the ship's cook, but found that a flexible interpretation of his duties extended to red-leading the holds and cleaning out the lavatories. Even the cooking was taxing; the mixed Portuguese, Scandinavian and Lascar crew demanded a catholic range of menus, and his ingenuity in conjuring up appetizing meals from unimaginative raw materials was kept constantly exercised. Failure to please brought swift retribution on a scale unknown even at Cheltenham. His one and only satisfied customer was the Greek nightwatchman, whose preferred diet was Kattomeat eaten straight from the tin. The ship's cat had to make do with scraps.

He signed off in New York, and with the money he had been able to save – his duties having permitted little shore leave – he bought a passage home on a luxury liner. His parents, although naturally pleased that he had returned safely, if not exactly on time, packed him straight off to the Westminster Technical Institute for Hotel Education, an establishment in which his father had taken a keen professional interest and of which, many years later, George would become a governor – the first ex-student to be appointed to such a post. Excused half of what was normally a three-year course because of his time at Lausanne, he galloped through the syllabus and then went off to the Continent to gain practical experience. After some time at the Kur in Bad Neuenahr (where William Cowpe was later also to train) he found his way to the most prestigious hotel in Germany, the Vierjahreseiten in Hamburg. In the course of a year as a *praktikant* (probationer) he spent a period in every department – kitchens, reception, dining room, even nightclub. He also became so proficient in German that he found himself saying his nightly prayers in the language.

In Hamburg, he met Etienne Vacher, then head of British Transport Hotels. Vacher liked what he saw and, being a close friend of OG, offered George a trainee managerial post in his organization. This new job took him from Germany first back to London, and then, in 1961, on to the Caledonian Hotel in Edinburgh, where he noticed for the first time how much American guests prized a private bathroom. The Caledonian, one of the most prestigious hotels in Scotland had, at that time, only one bath for every four bedrooms, and complaints in this respect were everyday occurrences. How lucky, he thought, that the Goring was better equipped. From Edinburgh he was posted to another BTH flagship, the Tregenna Castle in Cornwall, a move which was as agreeable as it was fortuitous, for it was there that he met Penny Williams.

Penny was running a riding stables with which the hotel had an arrangement and George, who knew nothing about horses other than that they appeared dangerous at both ends and uncomfortable in the middle, found himself spending every minute of his spare time in the yard. He decided that he would like to marry this diminutive, attractive brunette dynamo and, as she seemed to share his feelings, he set about breaking the good news to his parents. OG and Edna did not approve. This was no marriage for a man destined to be a leading light in the hotel industry. What George needed was not some farmer's daughter from the far south-west but a girl who, if not heir to one (or preferably more) of the better-known European hotel groups, was at least a close connection. OG had trawled the world in an effort to make such a match and, miraculously, Etienne Vacher had a daughter. And Etienne Vacher very much approved of George.

George was not to be deflected, however. Not only did he love Penny, he had seen in his parents too many disagreements that seemed to be the direct consequence of husband and wife both trying to run a single business. When his turn came, he was going to be the sole master, and Penny, he was sure, was never going to interfere. For one thing she hated London and for another she loved her work with horses too much to be parted from them for long. Perfect. In January 1962, four months after he left Vacher's employment to go to work for his father, he and Penny married. OG, acknowledging reluctantly that he had been outflanked, bought the couple a house in Chester Row, while Penny, anxious to get an equine foot in the door, moved a horse into the stables at Court Lodge. Slowly her in-laws grew to accept and then to like her; nine months later her first child, Theresa, was born, to be followed by Jeremy in 1966. They now needed a country home of their own and, disposing of their London house, bought Ruskins, also in Kent and not far from the Goring family home.

Life as an assistant manager was not easy. George was paid £35 a week and worked six full days, having only Saturday free. Banqueting, the cellar, staff wages and tradesmen's accounts formed the bulk of his duties, and Norman Pennington watched his every step, resenting this intrusion into a carefully established routine. OG was going through a period of debilitation from diabetes and spent little time at the Goring, preferring instead to concentrate on his outside professional interests and on manoeuvring his stocks and shares. When he did appear he found himself constantly at loggerheads with his son over repairs and renewals – George on the one hand feeling strongly that the hotel required a programme of almost complete redecoration and modernization, while OG took the view that, as occupancy rates remained at over 90 per cent, there was simply no need to spend money. For a time the old man had his way, in 1964 even buying the Spa Hotel in Tunbridge Wells for £100,000, with the aim of turning it into a country house hotel. The Spa was, to say the least, somewhat run-down, and huge amounts of money had to be raised to turn it into a marketable proposition. George in effect became its proprietor, overseeing a reconstruction which included moving the kitchens from the second floor to somewhere a little more accessible – an operation which put the newly formed Spa Hotel Goring Ltd into considerable debt. Before long, he came to realize that the family's new acquisition was best suited to the conference and banqueting trade, offering an imposing country-house air as well as a proximity to London which appealed to major companies. He therefore quickly abandoned plans to turn it into a rural replica of the Goring. In 1968, George became Managing Director, and Spa Hotel Goring remained one company until 1993 when he eventually separated the hotels, handing over full control at Tunbridge Wells to his brother Richard, who had sold up his building interests during the recession.

Back at the Goring, and by now with the full support of Pennington, George embarked on a modernization programme which touched every facet of the hotel. The public rooms, thanks to Edna's persistence, were just about acceptable; the bedrooms, cluttered with heavy dark furniture, and the bathrooms, with their Victorian plumbing still all too visible, were not. One by one the old fittings were rooted out and replaced with up-to-the-minute ones – all of the very best quality. As new beds arrived, George slept in each in turn to satisfy himself that they lived up to expectation, and thus earned for himself a paragraph in a national newspaper's gossip column headed 'Old George Sleeps Around!' The administrative systems, too, were automated for the first time, and staff pay and conditions placed on a basis more compatible with the second half of the twentieth century. Sick and holiday pay, pensions and other benefits were formalized to such a generous extent that the trade unions, who had begun to interest themselves in the Goring as a place likely to prove a

fruitful recruiting ground, were seen off in confusion. George agreed to a meeting between the staff and union representatives, and was gratified to hear that the Goring already exceeded, on every level, the advantages promised by union membership. The disappointed emissaries beat an undignified retreat when the meeting collapsed into general hilarity after some mischievous questions on gay rights – at that time not an issue high on the TUC's aggressively heterosexual agenda.

The sad deaths of both Norman Pennington and OG finally swept away the old guard. George now had his head and, with the enthusiastic assistance of William Cowpe, began to address the considerable problems caused by the London hotel slump of the 1970s. A government Grant and Loan scheme for the capital, promoted and administered by the British Tourist Board, had been introduced earlier, under the terms of which anyone building an hotel in London was offered an outright grant of £1,000 a bedroom. This and loans at favourable rates had led to an explosion of luxury hotels which far outstripped the demand. The situation was exacerbated by the increased threat of an IRA bombing campaign, and soon even the Goring's occupancy had dropped to an unprecedentedly low 70 per cent. Other grand hotels suffered more severely – 30 per cent rates were common – and most began to introduce a system of discounts in an effort to attract new trade. George would have none of this, taking the view that if anyone was to benefit from cut rates it should be his regular clients and not some casual visitor looking for a deal. The Goring had never given discounts, and his prices remained steadfastly unchanged. On one occasion a couple of chance visitors came into the hotel to ask the room rate, and when told pointed out forcibly that they had been offered a similar room at the Savoy for a great deal less. The reply was polite but uncompromising: 'That is true, sir. Enjoy your stay there. And when they put their prices up again, we shall still be here.'

George Goring's impeccably moral stance, although heartily approved by the regular guests who still formed the majority of his trade, did little for the overall finances of the hotel. He was forced to reconsider another of the Goring's traditions – that of refusing to pay agents to market the hotel. He saw no reason to compromise on this as far as the home trade was concerned but there was no doubt that agents in the United States, themselves struggling to persuade their clients to go to England, were increasingly unlikely to recommend the Goring for no payment to themselves, although they had done so for years knowing that their reputation would be enhanced by the service and atmosphere it offered. A solution recommended itself. Josephine Barr from Illinois had stayed at the Goring as a child, and had retained an affection for it which came close to being a love affair. She now ran the prestigious Barr Agency, and asked for a meeting. In 1981 George placed his hotel on her books, and for the first time the Goring had an agent – the last of London's grand hotels to succumb.

For twenty-five years George Goring, as Managing Director of Spa Hotel Goring Ltd, ran two hotels during which time each was extensively refurbished on rolling plans extending over ten years. Over the same period he was busily engaged in marketing both the Goring and the Spa – always very different establishments – through two severe recessions and, extraordinarily, in wiping out the debts incurred at the Spa. That he walked this tightrope successfully is an indication both of his acumen and a prodigious work-rate, which nevertheless still left him with the capacity to play a full part in the trade-related activities so beloved of his father and grandfather. Like them, he became prominent at a senior level in a number of professional associations, as well as gaining the presidency of the exclusive Réunion des Gastronomes. He was elected a Freeman of the City of London through his membership of the Distillers' and the Master Innholders', both ancient City livery companies, while his work as a governor of his old college in Westminster and his chairmanship of the Academy of Food and Wine Service (an organization devoted to the formal training of waiters) contributed to his being appointed to the OBE in the 1991 New Year's Honours List for 'Services to the hotel industry'. 'I don't think,' he said, when interviewed by a national magazine, 'that this means I'm a good guy, but it does mean that I run a jolly good hotel.'

Perhaps his most treasured professional achievement – because it signified the respect and admiration of his peers – was being elected Hotelier of the Year in 1990. 'If only I'd known you were coming, sir' said Peter Sweeney the doorman as he greeted, on the steps of the Goring, a man he knew to be one of the judges for this award, 'I'd have nominated Mr George as Hotelier of the Year this time round.' Little did Peter know that the guest he was joking with had in fact come to break the good news that very day.

OR and OG Goring left indelible impressions on the hotel world. OR would always be remembered as the pioneer who built an establishment that was the first in London to introduce comforts and conveniences that are now taken for granted. OG, in writing textbooks acknowledged widely as essential reading for aspiring hoteliers, and in his contributions to American magazines, did much to raise awareness of British standards of excellence at home and abroad. But neither man had significant interests outside the industry, and it is here that the third of the Gorings broke the mould. Apart from his hotel and his family, George developed two passions which he came to indulge as enthusiastically in middle age as he had as a younger man. The first and the most consuming is his love affair with horses and, in particular, those branches of equestrian sport which offer the most spectacular chances for him to break his neck.

It all started with Penny, who persuaded him that there was fun to be had away from the unremitting tarmac of London. She realized that her husband would need rather more of a challenge than trotting a hack round Hyde Park of a weekday morning, and introduced him to foxhunting. George took to the sport as a duck to water, and was soon out with local packs in Kent and Sussex. In search of more exciting country he took to hunting with the High Peak Harriers in Derbyshire, whose country is renowned for its wildness and its unforgiving stone walls – one of which caused him to fall so heavily that when he awoke, flat on his back, to see an anxious Prince of Wales bending over him with a flask of restorative brandy, he was able only to mutter 'Oh Lord, they'll never believe this at home.' But even the ruggedness of the High

gem of a horse he had acquired from Ireland, was soon to be known to all George's friends as Bugsy Alone.

It was natural, therefore, that when Bunn invented the sport of team chasing and introduced it at Hickstead in the mid-seventies, George and Bugsy should compete in the first event. Team chasing might have been (and possibly was) invented with George in mind. Teams of four ride across country against the clock over a variety of fences, both natural and man-made. For George it had everything: speed, danger, the 'haroosh' of the chase and, at the same time, the comradeship in which he revelled. The sport was, in short, wonderful and, with his brother Richard, he formed his own team, calling it 'The Boring Gorings' – their individual jerseys being emblazoned with 'Boring Old George', 'Boring Old Richard', and so on. Far from being boring, and setting new standards of apparently nerveless élan, they swept the board, winning events up and down the country. George and Bugsy invariably led the way and, if they managed to stay together, the Boring Gorings were always there or thereabouts among the prizewinners. Even if George occasionally dismounted involuntarily, Bugsy would go on by himself. On one such occasion George fell off at the first fence and Bugsy made equine history by taking every one of the twenty obstacles faultlessly without the benefit of any guidance from his forlorn would-be pilot. By this time George had learned enough about horsemanship to recognize his failings and had concluded that even when he was aboard, it was prudent to allow an animal of Bugsy's knowledge and experience to do his own thing. And he never carried a whip.

Bugsy Malone was lead horse for the Boring Gorings for fourteen years and even carried his master round the fearsome Pardubice Steeplechase in Czechoslovakia in 1983, finishing seventh out of forty-two starters and standing still while his rider remounted after a fall. He was still hunting – though now more gently, and partially retired – at the age of twenty-two. George, meanwhile, who is unlikely ever to recognize retirement for himself, later became enthused by a sport even more daunting than hunting or team chasing, and turned his attention to point-to-points. Anxious to gain experience quickly, and not able to race his own horses as often as he wished (his horses needing more rest than their owner), he took to accepting any ride that was offered to him by others. It was only slowly that he came to realize that such offers were often forthcoming because riders with a keener sense of self-preservation would not even consider them. He continued to fall a lot, and put up something of a record in taking part in well over a hundred point-to points without winning once. His own horse, Fortune's Fame, which did later win under other jockeys, came close to tarnishing this splendid series of glorious failures when, shouted on by an enthusiastic crowd of well-wishers, George took the lead approaching the last fence. Surely this time he would not be beaten? But Fortune's Fame who, unknown to his owner, disliked being in front quite so early, tried to run out through the wings of the fence, decanting his rider and breaking his leg for him in five places. This was enough even for George and he returned to hunting and the Boring Gorings, generously providing horses for his team-mates and, under the name of his hotel, sponsoring the annual National Team Chase Championships.

The equestrian activities to which George became addicted take place only in the winter months, leaving a prospect of long languid summers with nothing much to do on days off. Such idleness was clearly unacceptable, and he turned his attention to the water. Not for him, though, the gentle pleasures of sailing. Far too slow. What was needed was speed; something sporty to get him quickly across the Channel to his house in Brittany, and to play with off the north Cornish coast during his annual holiday at the family cottage near Port Isaac. It was no surprise that his approach to boats was taken at the same hair-raising pace which he demanded from his horses, and no surprise either that successive craft have all been named *Bugsy Malone*.

The first, a 16-foot flat-bottomed dory, was driven to the Isles of Scilly, to Alderney and to Cherbourg 'just to see what it was like'. What it was like came close to the terminal. Twice the first *Bugsy* sank and was resurrected; at the third attempt her owner wrote her off completely in mid-Channel. She was clearly not up to the job. The second *Bugsy* proved more durable, her 22-foot rigid inflatable frame driven along at gut-wrenching velocity by twin 140-horsepower engines. *Bugsy*

and her master, sometimes accompanied by unsuspecting friends (Penny went by ferry), criss-crossed the Channel with little regard for sea state or the closeness of isobars, and with her loaded down to her bloated gunwales with the good things of life. The arrangements, it was said, for keeping the Dom Pérignon cool, were a good deal more sophisticated than the navigational aids. George's one concession to those of a more nervous disposition was to dress his crew in bright orange 'Andy Pandy' suits, which keep out wind and rain but, more importantly, are clearly visible to the pilots of rescue helicopters.

He found *Bugsy Malone* the ideal craft for catching the fish he loves to cook – especially off the coast of France where his method remains both effective and highly original. Noticing that the boat looks very much like a French fisheries protection craft he goes in search of vessels trawling in illegal waters. Roaring up to them at speed, he enquires in his perfect French whether they have any fish to sell. The guilt-ridden captain, naturally assuming that this is a none too subtle attempt at the time-honoured Breton tradition of bribery, plays the game and tosses a couple of choice specimens of the day's catch into the bobbing *Bugsy*. George inspects his haul solemnly, nods, guns his engines puts them in gear. 'People sometimes wonder,' he muses innocently, 'how it is I catch so many beautiful turbot. I don't tell them, of course, but you couldn't do that in a sailing boat.'

The Royal National Lifeboat Institution, especially its branches in Cornwall, has watched *Bugsy*'s breakneck progresses through coastal waters with a close professional interest. The station at Port Isaac is usually put on full alert when its coxswain learns that Mr Goring is down for the weekend. As a sort of quid pro quo for this generous attention to his safety, the RNLI asked whether George might be persuaded to make a record-breaking run across the Irish Sea from Bude to Corkmacsherry as a fund-raising event. Apart from George, the boat would be crewed by lifeboatmen, thereby ensuring, by means of the powerful radios they carried, that rescue would be at hand if things went wrong. Always the philanthropist and ever keen to make his mark in the *Guinness Book of Records* (in December 1985 he and his nephew

Jonathan had become the first to cross from Dover to Calais on jet-skis), George enthusiastically agreed – with only the slightest twinge of regret when he realized that the date of the trip coincided with a visit by the Queen for luncheon at the Goring.

A considerable amount – around £60,000 – was raised but it was not until the day itself that George met his crew for the first time, being mildly surprised when he learned that three out of the four had never been offshore. This made him the undisputed expert and he asked to see the course that the RNLI had charted and approved. George did not approve. The sea state was slight but the forecast was none too good, and the route provided for *Bugsy* to hug the coast all the way to Fishguard in Wales before crossing St George's Channel at its narrowest point and then sticking to the Irish coast for the final leg. To the skipper this meant two things: firstly, he was being asked to spend far too much time inshore, where his experience told him that the forecast swells would be most dangerous, and secondly, there would be no chance of beating any records; they were being asked to travel much too far. Not good enough. He rewrote the script: they would head straight out to sea, contact the coastguard on Lundy Island as they passed to ask him to advise the RNLI of the changes, and then head for Cork like an arrow.

Things did not go quite to plan, however. *Bugsy*'s radio failed at the critical moment, and the RNLI's super-modern hand-held models failed to function at all. George took full responsibility; briefly consulting his newly installed satellite

navigation system, he opened up all 280 horsepower. Pausing in mid-channel to eat a picnic and ask a passing French ship to contact London, they sped on, making excellent time. At Corkmacsherry they received a hero's welcome from a pipe band and an enthusiastic crowd armed with an inexhaustible supply of Guinness.

In London, the top brass of the RNLI were less than happy. They had received no message, and the rescue services on both sides of the Irish Sea had been called out to search for what they imagined was a loss with all hands. When they were eventually able to interview the hapless lifeboatmen they disciplined them severely for allowing George to depart from the original plan. The latter protested in vain that it was his boat and his decision; he, and not they, were to blame. Furthermore, the trip had been completed successfully and had raised £60,000 for RNLI funds. 'I was buggered if I was going to put the whole thing in jeopardy by setting off on an impossible route as well as having to miss welcoming the Queen to the Goring.'

George Goring is a maverick who has won the respect and admiration of those who might have been expected only to be exasperated by his life-long devotion to flouting convention. Dapper in appearance (the word might have been coined for him), generous to a degree, determined always to be his own man, and with an entirely unassumed gift for the common touch, he illuminates the world of those fortunate enough to be affected by his multifarious activities. His impatience with red tape, coupled with an unrivalled professional reputation, led to his appointment to a government deregulation task force charged with unravelling some of the sillier attempts of the European Community to impose inappropriate legislation on the hotel industry. It is difficult to imagine someone more temperamentally suited to the job. His determination to fight off the attempts of national and international business groupings to buy the Goring – often at sums with so many appended noughts that they stagger his accountants – is born of the simple philosophy which also suffused his father and grandfather, and which is immutable: 'I do not want to be a Lord Forte or a bloody Trafalgar House, all I want to do is hand over a better hotel to my son than my father did to me. And I fully expect, in due course and because, God willing, there will always be a Goring at the Goring, that he will hand over a better hotel than I.'

That son is Jeremy. Born in 1966, educated at public school (but not Cheltenham!) followed by four years at Lausanne, he has been well groomed for his inheritance. Bilingual, widely travelled in the Far East, rock-and-roll drummer and trendy ex-nightclub owner, he too is his own man, determined from the start that, despite his father's plans, he alone will make his career decisions. Now, in 1997, the manager of a privately owned hotel in London which he describes as 'the only hotel in the world that is anything like the Goring', his mind is made up. When the call comes, he will be ready – the fourth of a direct line to take up the challenge of this, a very special place.